# *Holy Spirit*
# *for*
# *Healing*

# Also by Ron Roth, Ph.D.

## Books
(with Peter Occhiogrosso)

*The Healing Path of Prayer*
*Holy Spirit\**
*I Want to See Jesus in a New Light\**
*Prayer and the Five Stages of Healing\**

## Audios

*The Dark Night of the Soul\**
*Healing Prayers\**
*The Healing Path of Prayer*
*Holy Spirit: The Boundless Energy of God\**
*Prayer and the Five Stages of Healing\**
(two-tape and six-tape sets)\*

❧ ❧

(All of the above titles are available at your local bookstore.
Items with asterisks may also be ordered by calling
Hay House at 760-431-7695 or 800-654-5126.)

❧ ❧

Please visit the Hay House Website at: **hayhouse.com**
and Ron Roth's Website at: **ronroth.com**

# *Holy Spirit for Healing*

## Merging Ancient Wisdom with Modern Medicine

### Ron Roth, Ph.D.

with Peter Occhiogrosso

Hay House, Inc.
Carlsbad, California • Sydney, Australia

*Published and distributed in the United States by:*
Hay House, Inc., P.O. Box 5100, Carlsbad, CA 92018-5100 • (800) 654-5126
(800) 650-5115 (fax) • www.hayhouse.com

*Editorial Supervision:* Jill Kramer • *Design:* Summer McStravick

The author of this book does not dispense medical advice or prescribe the use of any technique as a form of treatment for physical or medical problems without the advice of a physician, either directly or indirectly. The intent of the author is only to offer information of a general nature to help you in your quest for emotional and spiritual well-being. In the event you use any of the information in this book for yourself, which is your constitutional right, the author and the publisher assume no responsibility for your actions.

**Library of Congress Cataloging-in-Publication Data**

Roth, Ron.
    Holy Spirit for healing : merging ancient wisdom with modern medicine / Ron Roth with Peter Occhiogrosso.
       p. cm.
    Includes bibliographical references.
    ISBN 1-56170-706-6
       1. Healing--Religious aspects--Christianity. 2. Holy Spirit.
    I. Occhiogrosso, Peter. II. Title.

BT732.2 .R68 2001
234'.131--dc21

                             00-065340

ISBN 1-56170-706-6

03 02 01 00    4 3 2 1
1st printing, February 2001

Printed in the United States of America

*To all the children of God,*
*and especially to my godchild, Eben Roth Odendaal,*
*daughter of Dawn Jiosi and Andries Odendaal.*

*"Every good and perfect gift is from above."*
James 1:17

# Contents

# Foreword

∽੭ ੮∾

*I*t is a privilege for me to add a few of my own thoughts to this treasure that Ron has created. When I sat down to read this manuscript, knowing Ron as well as I do and for as long as I have, I anticipated reviewing at least some familiar material. What I discovered is that I became fully engrossed in this text, and not just because his teachings are deeply insightful, but because they seem to communicate the Spirit itself. As I found myself being warmed inside, I forgot that I was reading Ron's book. I felt as though the energy of grace was coming into me. And then I thought, *Maybe I'm just reading this at the right time.* But I realized as soon as I said that to myself that there is no *wrong* time to read this.

Ron Roth is a genuinely ordained healer. I have observed him now for years, both as a teacher and as a healer, and I have watched as he silences himself before a healing and calls on the Holy Spirit to work through him. I have observed people in the audience release chronic physical pain or long-held traumatic memories. I know that this phenomenon is taking place because Ron has a healing rapport with the Holy Spirit, and when people are willing to welcome that grace into their lives, it comes.

As always, however, we cannot stay with the healer himself. Each of us must return to our own lives and face the challenges that fill the pages of life. The teachings and the exercises in this book will provide you with profound guidance on how to maintain your own process of healing and hope.

We are always healing in some way. It is not really accurate to say that we have been fully healed. That may be true of yesterday, of course, but there is always tomorrow. Tomorrow we will face even more obstacles that can shatter or weaken us. Tomorrow we will still have to remind ourselves to be grateful for our blessings. And tomorrow we will still have to continue to pray and be with our own spirit. Healing is a practice, a spiritual discipline unto itself. It requires self-examination, prayer, and conscious choice. Ron Roth has provided a guidebook in the writing of this text that I believe to be a genuine vessel for calling forward the power of the Holy Spirit into our lives.

Even though Ron and I have been close friends for many years, I am still amazed by his healing charisma with people. Perhaps no one ceases to be amazed by the power of the Holy Spirit manifested.

— Caroline M. Myss, Ph.D., author of
*Anatomy of the Spirit* and
*Why People Don't Heal and How They Can*

# Introduction

‿ა ‿ა

## Signs and Wonders

*C*ertain theologians have been saying for some time that
what Jesus did when he walked the earth was not
really miraculous at all. In the Greek Scriptures, they
point out, the word *miracle* does not appear as it does in some
of our English translations. The term we translate as *miracles*
actually means in Greek something closer to "signs and wonders." These events were signs that made people wonder what
Jesus was all about. They were miracles to those who were
unaware or not knowledgeable. But because Jesus was thinking with the mind of God, he was able to understand laws of
the universe—laws of physics and science—that we have
never fully understood and still don't, which is why we call
them "miracles." Rather than resisting these theologians
because they are challenging cherished assumptions and
beliefs, we can use their insights to help us focus on what is
genuinely significant in the Gospel accounts. Seen in that vein,
Jesus is actually saying, "You are all sons and daughters of
the living God, and what I can do, so can you."

What I would like to get across to you in this book is not
so much how to *heal* others, but how to take care of your *own*
health. Once you fully and deeply experience self-healing,
you can share it with others. What helps you learn healing
methods quickly is practicing them on yourself. When I
applied these prayer principles and affirmations to myself—

to settle down the diabetes that was beginning to overtake me years ago, to alleviate the arthritic problems that were beginning to attack my hand, or when a lump began to grow under my arm—I learned more about how these methods work than when I served as a vehicle for healing others. To begin with, I started to take the time to pray and meditate and practice the discipline I was teaching others.

If you crave wholeness, if you want to live life abundantly, you must have desire, determination, and discipline. So many times when people come to me for help and are instantaneously healed, they go to the doctor and are told that they've gone into remission. Then they make the mistake of abandoning their fledgling spiritual practice and awareness and go back to their old way of living, *without* prayer and meditation. That would be like having a quadruple bypass operation, and then getting out of the hospital and eating fast food and smoking cigarettes again because—hey, you're healed!

### Good Stress, Bad Stress

We have to realize that although some healings are instantaneous, most come about by adhering to laws that regulate healing, health, and healthy relationships. The principles set down in the sacred Scriptures will make our life abundant and meaningful—but only if we practice them. Becoming familiar with the methods and practicing them regularly can help stop what I call our yo-yo existence, the experience of feeling "on" one day and "off" the next. Too many human beings live a roller-coaster life driven by their emotions and the vagaries of the mind, which is a notorious rambler.

What I teach doesn't mean that your life will be totally stress free, nor do you want it to be, because although negative stress can have disastrous effects on your emotions and health, positive stress is good. The difference between the two is the difference between living under what one bodyworker I know calls "I will" power instead of "I can" power. When you have to will yourself to get something done "no matter what," you end up draining energy from your system. If you're constantly pushing yourself, working 12 to 14 hours a day without any downtime just to meet a deadline, make your boss happy, or buy a big new home for your family, you're accumulating negative stress.

Positive stress comprises the creative tension you feel when working on a project that excites you. When you're in demand and feel a sense of mastery, everybody wants your services and you get to pick and choose what's best for you. A single mother facing the challenge of raising her kids while earning a living may feel positive stress, but if she isn't careful, it can degenerate into negative stress. Sometimes we have to make a conscious decision to cut down on our needs and expenses so that we can work less. I recently read about a woman in the Seattle area who chose to stay home to raise her children rather than supplementing her husband's income with a career of her own. This meant living in a smaller house, not buying a new gas-guzzling sport utility vehicle, and sometimes not knowing if her checks would bounce. For her it wasn't a matter of being politically correct or returning to a more traditional way of life. It was simply doing what she felt in her heart—in her inner self—was the right thing for her and her family. She acknowledged that she experienced some stress in her life, but I would consider it positive stress— the stress of facing a challenge and meeting it with courage and resourcefulness.

Although most people don't think of spiritual practice in terms of stress, the beginning stages can be very stressful. You don't know if you're doing it right, and you don't really know what to expect if you do. But that's also a kind of positive stress, like being ten years old and wondering if you're going to get that chemistry set you want for your birthday. Eventually, if you keep at it, your body rewards you by releasing all kinds of good feelings and positive sensations. Think of an athlete training for a marathon, pushing herself to run farther every week. That may seem like stress to a lot of people—especially the couch potatoes among us—and on a certain physical level, it *is* stressful. But again, the body rewards you by releasing endorphins that uplift you and fill you with positive energy.

The only danger arising from that kind of positive stress is the tendency to want to stay on the mountaintop because you get addicted to the endorphin release. The meditator decides to meditate 20 hours a day, or the marathoner spends all her spare time running, to the detriment of work or family life. I have even heard the story of one born-again Christian who became so captivated by the "high" of communicating with fellow believers in a Christian chat room on the Internet that he wasn't spending enough time with his wife and son, and his marriage began to suffer. His wife had to confront him at a church meeting, and the other members of the congregation had to convince him that you really can have too much of a good thing. The other danger in getting addicted to the blissful feelings that can stem from prayer and meditation is that you may begin to believe that you should *always* feel that way. So when a period of aridity comes, you may be discouraged and quit altogether. The saints experienced stress of a different kind. They put all their eggs in one basket, and when they entered the dark night of the soul, feeling that God was absent or distant from them, they could fall into deep despair.

Even Padre Pio, the great 20th-century Italian mystic, had fits of depression and despondency, as though God had abandoned him. In the early years, he became obsessed with the need for purification of the senses to contemplate God more fully. When I was young, I also spent a lot of time in prayer and meditation, and if things started to go wrong, I'd run to church—not to seek God, but to find answers. One thing that has impressed me about both the Christian and Hindu mystics is their understanding that you do not meditate to "get" anything, but only to know God. Yogananda always said that you could not approach meditation with the idea of receiving something in return. You go to *find* God, and then anything that results—whether it's increased insight, peacefulness, inner strength, or a more coherent life—is gravy. Most of us start out trying to get the good results first, and God is just a fringe benefit.

So as you work your way through this book, be aware of the fine line between the positive stress that stems from doing spiritual work and releases spiritual endorphins, and the negative stress that may develop from going to extremes. What is most important is to remember that you don't have to get rid of *all* stress in your life. The only people I know who have done that are six feet under. It's much better to learn to live with an *acceptable* level of stress, just as you learn to live with change and growth. The only alternative is stagnation and spiritual stultification.

# Chapter One

❧

# We Are Wondrously Made

*T*he first step in healing is to convince ourselves that God loves us, and that He always cares for us. When we get ill, we often think, *God has laid this sickness on me. God has caused this suffering in my life because I deserve to be punished.* But you don't find that sentiment anywhere in the teachings of Jesus. When Jesus encountered the man blind from birth (John 9), his disciples asked him, "Rabbi, who sinned, this man or his parents, that he was born blind?"

"Neither this man nor his parents sinned," Jesus replied, "but that the works of God should be revealed in him."

God deeply desires good things for us, as stated clearly in Jeremiah 29:11: "For I know the plans I have for you," declares the Lord, "plans to prosper you and not to harm you, plans to give you a future and a hope." The next time something goes wrong in your life, from a small slipup to a major disappointment, see if you don't say, based on your past programming, "God must want me to learn a lesson." That implies that something negative is occurring and God is "doing it to you." Not that God can't use sickness to redirect our lifestyle. He can use *anything,* but let's stop blaming Him. When we get a cold, most of us get into bed and say, "This has got to run its course." That is the equivalent of saying, "I am a victim in this."

Because realizing how we are made will make us more

aware of God's love and His grand design for our lives, I direct your attention to Psalm 139:14ff, in which the Psalmist is addressing God. Most translations use the word *fearfully* in the opening verse, but the original is closer to *awful* (in the sense of "full of awe or wonder") or *awesome*.

> *I praise you because I am wondrously made.*
>     *O Lord, your works are wonderful.*
> *You know me full well; my frame was not hidden from*
>     *you when I was made in the secret place, when I was*
>     *woven together in the depths of the earth.*
> *Your eyes saw my unformed body.*

### The Mind/Body Connection

The human being is designed for health, not sickness. But to understand how to achieve health, we first have to know a little bit about how the human body works, and about the interrelationship of the mind and the body. Then we can chart the role played by the Holy Spirit in healing and wholeness.

When the fetus is growing in the womb, the first organ to begin developing is the brain. The brain can best be described as a wondrously made machine, a sophisticated living computer composed of ten billion cells called *neurons* that never sleep. It receives and interprets electrochemical impulses through more than 500 trillion connections called *synapses*. The brain is the master of the body.

The body has more than 100,000 miles of tubing that carries blood throughout our system. Some vessels are so small that we didn't know they were there until the microscope was invented. The bloodstream is also a repair system, capable of rushing red and white cells to any part of our body in great numbers, and is able to produce approximately ten million red cells every second. Be in awe of your body so that you will take responsibility for caring for this magnificent machine.

We now know that over the course of a year or so, most of the body's cells are replaced, and about every three years, all the cells in the body except brain cells are replaced. Isn't that magnificent? As one example of the body's miraculous functioning, we just have to look at what happens when it's threatened with infection. Once a virus becomes active in our body, the signal is flashed to our brain, which, acting like a computer, dispatches defensive forces to fight the virus. An army of antibodies is raised and mobilized, and the organism is ready to battle the invader.

If the body is so wonderful, then, why do we still get sick? Some people assume that God inflicts illness and disease upon us, and they wonder why. But God does *not* send us sickness; we often bring it about in our own lives by our reactions to people and situations and by our negative thought patterns. That raises the question of children who are born with a disease or sickness or some deformity. Surely they are too young to have developed negative thought patterns. Yet sometimes when there's a traumatic experience in the life of the mother carrying the fetus, continued fear or anger caused by an abusive or absent father, or a conflict about whether to have the baby or not, those negative emotions may be passed on to the child much as the physical manifestations of alcohol or drug abuse or malnutrition are passed on. And for those who believe in the laws of karma and reincarnation, the seeds of actions committed in a previous life may bear fruit in this one.

Whenever I talk about illness or disease arising from actions in the past—either in this life or a previous one—I am careful to point out that we should avoid dwelling on them in a way that induces guilt. Guilt always relates to the past, and even illness must be experienced in this present moment. If guilt crops up, get rid of it. I will show you how in the exercise that follows. At the same time, it's damaging to speculate about illness or disease in others. Keep in mind the words of Jesus that I quoted at the beginning of this chapter: "Neither this man nor his parents sinned, but that the works of God should be revealed in him." A variety of factors leads to illness—including diet, environment, and genetic predisposition—but negative thought patterns can be the weight that tips the balance.

### Exercise: Healing Guilt Through the Holy Spirit

Although guilt is such a destructive force in our lives, its very ubiquity often makes us unaware that we are even feeling guilty, or that guilt can be counteracted. But like all negative emotions, the more we give in to it, the more it becomes a reflex action. Over the years, I've developed a seven-step approach to healing guilt in collaboration with the Holy Spirit. You don't have to follow the steps in strict order every time you experience guilt; it's enough to keep them in mind and use as many of them as you can to alleviate the negativity and pain associated with guilt.

1. Begin by humbly accepting responsibility for where you are at the present moment. If you've done something that has induced guilt, acknowledge it without necessarily blaming yourself.

2. Now, take three deep breaths and visualize Jesus (or Mary, Tara, the Buddha, Lao-tzu, Ramakrishna, or any deity or holy being with whom you feel a special connection) embracing you as if you were a little child longing to be held and loved.

3. Acknowledge your weaknesses and ask the Holy Spirit to fill you with Her strength. Be as brave and courageous as you are able.

4. Ask the Spirit to heal you of whatever in you needs healing. Then become quiet and listen closely to any thoughts, hunches, or ideas that may come to you. They represent the pathway to your healing.

5. Forgive whatever and whomever you need to forgive, including yourself. Remember that forgiveness does not mean that you condone the behavior in question— even your own. It simply means that you release it to the Spirit of God.

6. Allow the healing love of the Divine Father-Mother to flow throughout your entire being. Visualize it as a white or golden light if you wish, and invite it to enter your body through the crown of your head and flow down through your heart center into your entire system.

7. Commit yourself to a new positive form of motivation and action. This can be as simple as becoming aware of any negative thoughts you feel about yourself and letting go of them. Your next commitment might be to learn more about spiritual principles and ways to apply them to your life through listening to audiotapes, reading books, attending workshops, and doing spiritual exercises (including this one) on a regular basis. As I wrote in *Prayer and the Five Stages of Healing*, negative thoughts and emotions take on a life and a momentum of their own. Eastern Orthodox mystics often refer to that accumulated energy as "negative elementals," and believe that the more we indulge these negative energies, the more they accumulate around us and predispose us to becoming even more negative. Someone who never tries to control his temper will find it easier and easier to fly into a rage, and the rages

may become more destructive with time. Your goal should be to create a positive momentum rather than a negative one.

You can close this session by taking a deep breath and expressing gratitude for whatever is happening within, even if you don't feel anything immediately. Energy is never completely static; it is always moving in some direction, although we may not be aware of it.

## Programming for Health

The Third Letter of John says, "Beloved, I pray that you may prosper and be in good health, even as your inner being prospers and is in good health." John knew that the power to heal is *within* us, not *outside* of ourselves. We can make use of things outside of us, such as medicine and counseling, but healing begins inside each of us with a desire to be the best person we can be. There are only two basic reactions to anything that happens to us in life: It can make us *bitter,* or it can make us *better.*

When we persist in unhealthy thinking, we install sickness programming into the computer program of our brain, which is the subconscious or the unconscious. The subconscious is designed to activate by the law of belief. The Book of Proverbs of the Old Testament or Hebrew Bible says (23:7), "As one thinks in his heart, so is he." The Buddha said almost precisely the same thing some 500 years after the material from which this part of Proverbs derives was written but at least five centuries before Christ (*Dhammapada,* 1-2):

*All states have mind as their forerunner, mind is their chief, and they are mind-made. If one speaks or acts with a defiled mind, then suffering follows one even as the wheel follows the hoof of the draft-ox. . . . If one speaks or acts with a pure mind, happiness follows as one's shadow that does not leave one.*

And in the Book of Deuteronomy (30:19-20), the Lord says, "This day I call heaven and earth as witnesses against you. I have set before you life and death, blessings and curses; now choose life, so that you and your children may live and that you may love the Lord your God, listen to His voice and hold fast to Him." You may say that you didn't choose to lose your job, that you didn't want that at all. On a conscious level, you may not have; but on a subconscious level, you have chosen it based on your programming.

Until perhaps a decade ago, I had the most horrible time losing weight. Then I realized that I kept seeing a picture in my mind of "Fat Little Ronnie." Around the same time, I learned the following sequence of events leading from cause to effect:

1. Programming creates beliefs.
2. Beliefs create attitudes.
3. Attitudes create feelings.
4. Feelings determine action.
5. Action creates results.

Let's examine those one at a time:

— **Programming creates beliefs.** How we were programmed early in life goes a long way toward creating our current beliefs. All the negative thoughts and emotions that your mother experienced while you were in the womb, the conflicts between your parents while you were growing up, the extent to which they belittled or demeaned or discouraged you, have all gone into creating the backlog of negative thoughts and feelings in your body today.

**— Beliefs create attitudes.** One aspect of my work is a process called *the healing of memories.* That doesn't mean your memories are healed and gone. The memory remains, but every memory that is negative has a negative energy, a sting, attached to it. When that memory is evoked, all the emotion that occurred back then, even if it was 30 years ago, is still in your system. When older people hear certain songs, they think of someone who did them wrong when they were teenagers. A headache occurs, and they wonder where it came from, but the toxic poison of an earlier hurt is still in their system. Healing memories is about healing the *sting,* not the memory itself.

**— Attitudes create feelings.** People often end up in disastrous relationships because on a subconscious level they still don't believe that they deserve better, so they keep getting exactly what they believe they deserve. When that happens, it's time to change your thinking. In a sense, that's what used to be meant by the word *repent,* which, unfortunately, has taken on terribly negative connotations. The Greek word *metanoia,* which is translated as "repent," actually means "to change your thinking." When Jesus said, "Repent and believe," he was telling people to change their thinking so that they could believe in the good news. Today we might call that *reprogramming* or *reframing.*

**— Feelings determine action.** We act, for better or worse, on the basis of feelings over which all too often we have little control. This is where you need to bring in the Holy Spirit and ask the Spirit to show you what is causing you to act this way—but then you have to do something about it. So many times people will call me and say, "Pray that I have peace of mind." I can't! That is something you must bring to pass in your own life. I can pray, however, that maybe you'll get sick enough so that you won't want the life you have anymore, but want peace of mind instead. I know that other spiritual healers say they will pray for your peace of mind because they don't want to hurt your feelings. But I feel that I have to tell you the truth. Some things are up to *you* to do, which is why Paul, in his Letter to the Ephesians, advocates getting rid of the rage in your heart. You can't ask God to get rid of your rage for you. God will help you recognize it, but then *you* have to go to work on it.

— **Actions create results.** That process is going on in each of our lives, leaving us to ask some good questions of ourselves: *What do I really want? What do I think I really deserve?* You may think you want to be healthy, but a subconscious vibration is asking: *Do I deserve to be healthy?*

Once I understood the sequence I've just enumerated, I began to imagine myself the way I believed I was meant to be. At the height of a seemingly endless struggle with being overweight, I noticed that often I wasn't hungry and didn't need to eat, but would do so out of habit. I decided that whereas I used to make ten trips to the refrigerator in the course of a day, I could make seven, then five, then three. Do I still have binges at times? Sure, but not every day. We can change our belief system from negative to positive, and we can believe about ourselves what God says is true about us. He created man and woman and said, "It is good."

Throughout your life, you may have heard from different sources—parents, teachers, bosses, abusive or aggrieved lovers or spouses—that you're worthless, a worm, no good, evil. When you think of all the times such things have been said to you from childhood on, you begin to see how determined you have to be to counteract the power those statements can hold over your psyche. You need to make it the number-one desire in your life to change all that, and although it's possible, it takes discipline. Some behavioral psychologists say that for every negative thought implanted in our minds, we need ten positive thoughts to reprogram it. Sometimes I think that it should be more like 100 or 1,000.

Due to the backlog of negative thoughts that remain in my subconscious even today, after years of interior work, I make use of positive video- and audiocassettes in the morning and evening two or three times a week. Before leaving home to give a workshop, I may listen two or three hours during the day, and I can feel the difference in my spirit when I get up in the morning after a week of listening. I also listen to classical music in the background much of the day, because it has a soothing and regulating effect on my psyche.

Programming takes place in our conscious mind. You can feed into the conscious mind what you want programmed into your subconscious, but you have to do it *with feeling*. You have to show determination and discipline. Ask yourself if you want to continue to feel negative or if you're ready to change. I came to a point in my life where I said, "This is a hell of a way to live." I was blaming everybody else—every situation and circumstance that had ever occurred in my life— for feeling miserable and frustrated and angry. I wanted to find a *heavenly* way to live. In the Gospel of Mark (7:14-23), Jesus tells the people, "There is nothing outside of a man that by going into him can defile him; but the things which come out of a man are what defile him." After he leaves the crowd, his disciples ask him to explain this parable.

"Are you so dull?" Jesus replies, apparently incredulous that they don't get his point. "Don't you see that nothing that enters a man from the outside can make him unclean?" Jesus wanted to shift the focus in the religion of his day from ritual dietary cleanliness to a spiritual inner purity that transcends religion. He is saying that food, which enters the body from the outside, cannot make one unclean, for it doesn't go into the heart, or the inner being, but into the stomach, and then out of the body in a very short time. "What comes out of a man is what makes him unclean," Jesus continues. "For from within, from out of the heart of man, come evil thoughts, sexual misconduct, theft, murder, adultery, greed, malice, deceit, envy, slander, arrogance." These are all forms of negativity. In translating this passage, the Living Bible astutely paraphrases: "It is man's thought life that pollutes."

The converse is also true: Out of the heart, out of the mind, out of the inner being good can flow. In Romans 12:2, Paul writes: "Do not conform any longer to the pattern of this world but be transformed by the renewing of your mind. Then you will be able to attest and approve what God's will is, His good, pleasing and perfect will." The pattern of this world is, in essence, negative thinking. By this world, Paul means concern with appearances, which is still true today. If you turn on the news, you will see primarily negative events—fires, accidents, murders, political intrigue, and scandals. Even the weather forecast will be negative! If they tell you that there's a 20 percent chance of rain or snow, that means there's an 80 percent chance it will be clear. And just about every advertisement you will ever see is trying to convince you that there's something wrong with you: Your breath is offensive, your body smells, your house is a mess, your clothes aren't sexy enough, your car is outmoded—even your dog food is second-rate.

After watching the news and commercials all our lives, does it seem odd that we begin to think negatively about ourselves? We've all experienced getting a good idea and then hearing ourselves say, *Oh, that's wonderful! That really excites me . . . but I can't do that.* You want to do it, but you can't. You really believe you can't—and I'm speaking from my own personal experiences.

The brain is in touch with every part of the body through countless miles of nerves, which, along with every cell in the body, are under the direct control of the brain. A segment of skin the size of a postage stamp contains about four yards of nerves. Information about that bit of skin races along nerves to the brain at the rate of 300 miles per hour. Our organs are automatically regulated by the brain via the autonomic nervous system (ANS). If I want a glass of water, my conscious mind gives the command, and my hand reaches for the glass and the tap. But once I put the glass to my lips, it's completely out of my control. My ANS directs the process from the subconscious area of the brain. Wherever the ANS carries messages from the brain, it's possible for symptoms to appear. Since every organ in the body is linked to the brain, then every organ can become the target of emotional abuse. Everything from poor eyesight to sexual dysfunction can result from the destructive thoughts that we picture in our minds.

The body is not designed to handle the powerful negative emotions of guilt, fear, and hate. Such strong emotions have to be discharged somewhere, and once the subconscious area of the brain selects an organ of the body as the whipping boy for a particular emotional problem, that choice is entered into the body's computer system, the subconscious. After that, every time those same feelings occur and have to be disposed of, the stress will be directed against that same organ. We can't consciously choose which organ will be the target for these emotions, although there does seem to be a general pattern of favorite targets for particular emotions, as Louise Hay pointed out in her first book, *Heal Your Body*. In a later work, Hay explained that this book "began as a simple list of metaphysical causations for physical illnesses in the body." Just to take one example, she connects problems in the neck and throat area with an inability to be flexible and to speak up for ourselves. "The neck represents the ability to be flexible in our thinking, to see the other side of a question, and to see another person's viewpoint." An ailment of the neck, she concludes, "usually means that we are being stubborn about our own concept of a situation." Problems such as sore throats and laryngitis indicate unexpressed anger that make it difficult to speak, whereas tonsillitis and thyroid conditions "are just frustrated creativity, resulting from not being able to do what you want to do."

When we experience worry and anxiety, or when we allow bitterness and discontentment to persist in our minds, we may invite sickness into the body. The stress doesn't have to come in a mighty surge, but can be a steady pounding, hour after hour, day after day, month after month. When you learn to pray positively and acquire the powerful miracle-working manifestations of decree and blessing, that pounding eventually fades away.

The good news is that, because we're wondrously made by God, the body does also respond favorably to the positive emotions of love, tenderness, affection, appreciation, peace, joy, and humor. Doctors and scientists have been doing experiments for the past few decades on plants and animals, laying hands on them and finding that dying plants, for instance, come back to life. God has placed within us His Spirit, which is healing energy, and we have to become aware of how to utilize that Spirit for the greatest impact on our lives and the lives of our loved ones.

Some years ago, I was asked to come to Connecticut to lay hands on a woman named Sylvia who had seen me at a workshop in Philadelphia. At the time, she had suffered from chronic backaches for more than 20 years, and during the service, as I was holding a little boy in my arms who was eventually healed of leukemia, Sylvia was knocked to the floor. When she got up, she was pain free and never had a backache again.

But now, Sylvia wanted me to help her husband, Jack. I said I would come to Connecticut, but that I couldn't guarantee anything.

When I arrived and began to pray with Jack, I said nothing. I just put my hands on his back as I was led to do, even though he had cancer in the lungs, and thought only of love, peace, and joy. Occasionally he said, "Ron, it's getting hotter. God, I feel so good." He was to start his chemotherapy in a couple of days, and I told him not to program his mind with the standard expectation that his hair would fall out and he'd throw up and lose his appetite and be miserable for two weeks afterwards. Although the husband and wife were both Jewish, I suggested that he put on the mind that was in Jesus Christ. He looked at me, laughed, then said, "It's okay, I understand what you mean."

I told Jack not to concentrate on the needle, which was how he would receive his treatments, but to see the doctor's hand full of light, see the needle full of light, see the fluid in the needle full of light. "When he puts it into your vein," I said, "see nothing but light passing through your vein. That's the energy of God. Keep telling yourself that's the energy of God, and the energy of God cannot make you sick."

During his entire chemotherapy treatment, Jack never became sick. Even the doctor warned him that he would probably get sick, but this guy just looked up and said, "No, I won't." He came home and had a wonderful party that night, and ate a lot of his wife's cooking.

The cancer went into remission, but there's a disturbing coda to this story. Jack had built a beautiful home for his wife and himself in a well-to-do area of New England that was worth easily three-quarters of a million dollars, but Sylvia wanted to move to Florida. He was against leaving Connecticut because he still had his business there, was making very good money, and liked the people. But Jack usually did what his wife wanted, so they began to plan their move. About a year after I worked with Jack, I got a phone call. The cancer wasn't a problem, but he had died suddenly of a heart attack just before they were to leave for Florida. To this day, I'm convinced that the impending move created so much tension in Jack that his heart finally gave out.

## The Pathway to Healing

Many years ago when I was first becoming aware of the unresolved anger and bitterness still lodged within me from childhood, I asked the Holy Spirit to show me the pathway to healing. I was getting a distinct message that I needed to clear some issues around what had occurred at the ages of 7 and 13, but I knew I would have to have help resolving them. Around that time, I began to receive flyers in the mail for tapes and workshops by John Bradshaw, whom I had not really been aware of before. But I took them as a cue, and when I saw that he was going to be appearing on public television giving a workshop based on one of his best-selling books about healing childhood traumas, called *Homecoming*, I made sure to watch. Bradshaw more or less pioneered the concept of the "inner child" and brought the term "dysfunctional family" into everyday use. I liked that he had *lived* everything he spoke about, and I could relate to the fact that, like me, he had an alcoholic father and had studied for the Catholic priesthood. I also appreciated the fact that he was coming from a spiritual perspective yet seemed like an ordinary guy, and I fell in love with his teachings.

I don't even know how I got on the mailing list for those Bradshaw flyers, but after I watched the show, I was so moved that I ordered the whole set of videocassettes. I worked through those tapes twice, and I got the answers to my questions about what had happened to me at ages 7 and 13. That was my pathway to emotional healing and the start of seriously building my self-esteem. It didn't come directly from the Holy Spirit—it came from John Bradshaw. And yet I know the Spirit was working by cuing me with those flyers, as well as the opportunity to see this man on TV without even leaving my house.

This is what I mean when I say that the mind must be controlled by the Spirit, and the body controlled by the mind.

The Spirit can guide us toward the pathway to healing, but we may have to make some purchases and exert some effort along the way. The key is putting our lives under the guidance of the Spirit to discover where the healing needs to take place in our lives.

# Chapter Two

❧

# The Power of Decree

*A*uthentic prayer has three components. The first is referred to in Christianity as *the Holy Spirit,* which I will call *the Spirit of Wholeness* or the "still, small voice" that Elisha heard in the Old Testament. We need to learn how to listen to this inner voice, to know that prayer isn't just about talking, but is also, perhaps predominantly, about listening. It isn't a monologue, but a Divine dialogue between you and the essence of your being. You talk *and* you listen. That Divine Essence within talks, and that Divine Essence listens.

The second component of authentic prayer is faith. By that I don't mean doctrine or dogma or faith in the church. Real faith is the energy to command—the faith that is talked about by mystics and yogis and adepts of all traditions as the boundless energy that comes from believing that Divine potential resides in each of us.

The third component is what the mystics understood by prayer. As I have noted in previous books, the ancient languages of Sanskrit and Aramaic have no one word that translates literally as *prayer* in our sense of the term. The traditional Western concept of prayer is a monologue of asking or begging because we really don't believe that we deserve what we want. In Sanskrit, the word that comes closest to *prayer* is *pal al,* which means "seeing yourself as wondrously made."

And the word that comes closest to *prayer* in Aramaic is *slotha*, which means "to set a trap," implying that when we wish to communicate with the Divine Essence that fills the whole universe, we leave ourselves open, like a hunter's snare, to catch the thoughts of God.

Recall for a moment the statement of Jesus in the Gospel of Luke (17:6): "If your faith were only the size of a mustard seed," Jesus answered, "you could say to this mulberry tree, 'be uprooted and planted in the sea,' and it would obey you." Years ago when I was studying theology in graduate school, one of our professors told us a remarkable story about Carl Jung, the great psychoanalyst. He said that Jung believed in the mysteries of the sacred writings and Divine intervention, which we call miracles, yet which are not miracles at all in the way some people understand them.

When Jung was asked to discuss what he believed about God and miracles, he would often tell the story of the rainmaker. It seems that a certain village in Europe was entering the fifth year of a terrible drought. For four years they had suffered enormously, and there wasn't a drop of rain anywhere on the land. They tried to find rainmakers to come and produce rain for them, but everything they tried failed. Then one day, the village heard about a great rainmaker in a nearby country who could produce rain without fail. So they went to find this man and brought him back to their village. As he entered the village, he stopped, looked around, pitched a tent, and went into the tent for four days. Nobody saw him during that time, but on the fifth day, the rains came in torrents, a deluge.

The people were ecstatic. They were jumping up and down, exclaiming how wonderful it was. Of course, the rainmaker came out of his tent to join in the celebration. They began to ask him what he had done to bring the rain.

The rainmaker looked puzzled. "What do you mean, what did I do?"

"Look at how it's raining!" they exclaimed. "Nobody else has ever been able to do this."

The rainmaker looked at them and very humbly said, "I have done nothing."

This only startled the people more. "What do you mean, you did nothing? You came to our village and after four days, the rains began to fall. Please tell us what you did."

"All right," he said, "let me tell you. When I came here, the first thing I noticed is that the whole village was out of harmony with God. I went into the tent and got in harmony with God, and then the rains came."

When I heard this story, my first question was, *How did he pray? How did he get into harmony?* I didn't realize that there were already instances in my own life when things that seemed to be coincidental were occurring. We often think that prayer is a hit-or-miss affair: Sometimes God likes you and does what you ask, and sometimes He doesn't like you, so He *doesn't* do what you want. We have to acquire a more sophisticated understanding of the principles of authentic prayer and begin to work with them.

Implicit in the second component enumerated above is that faith is an energy to command. Most of us shrink at that thought, as if it means that we're commanding God. But we're using the God-spirit within us to command the negative energies that are harassing us to get out of our lives once and for all. When I learned that, everything in my life changed. As I learned to line up my emotions with my thoughts and feelings, my spiritual life grew by leaps and bounds. The secret behind that energy is an ancient form of prayer known as *decree*, and it's one of the most powerful healing forces you can use. To understand how decree has been employed in the past, a little background is in order.

You may have read the following scriptural story before, but it has probably been channeled through your mind and your mind's belief that prayer is about asking and begging, because God is withholding something from you. You may believe that God is the great withholder, and you've got to twist His arm to get an answer. In his Letter (5:14), James writes: "Is anyone among you sick? He should call in the church elders, the spiritual guides, and they should pray over him, anointing him with oil in the name of the Lord. The prayer of faith will save the sick person and the Lord will raise him up again. . . . The heartfelt prayer of someone upright works very powerfully."

James goes on to say how you can build up this kind of faith, which is the energy to command, by briefly summarizing the story of Elijah that appears in the Hebrew Testament. "Elijah was a man of like nature with ourselves and he prayed earnestly that it might not rain, and for three years and six months, it did not rain on the earth. Then he prayed again, and the heaven gave forth rain, and the earth brought forth its fruit." The story of Elijah as told in 1 Kings, chapter 17, goes like this:

> *Elijah, the Tishbite, of the temporary residence of Gilead, said to Ahab and decreed, "As the Lord God of Israel lives, before whom I stand, there shall be neither dew nor rain these coming years unless I give the word."*

Elijah knew his authority; he knew he was a child of the Divine. *The Spirit of the living God is at the core of my being,* he said to himself, *and if I hear it's not going to rain, I know it's not going to rain, and I'm going to decree that it's not going to rain.*

Does that fit in with the way you were taught to pray earnestly?

So the skies stopped, and it didn't rain for three and a half years. Then, in 1 Kings 18:41, Elijah said to Ahab, "Go up, eat and drink; for there is a sound of the abundance of rain." Nothing in those chapters shows Elijah saying to the Lord, "Oh, please, send rain." Nor does Elijah bargain with God.

He doesn't say, "I'll do what you want, God, if you let it rain. I'll fast for 40 days. Do your part and I'll do mine."

That may be the way *we* were taught, but it's not the way of spiritual wisdom. That way says that you know who you are and what your potential is. You know that with the presence of God, you can do anything.

In the Gospel of Mark (11:12-25), Jesus approaches a fig tree that is in leaf and looks to see if it has any fruit on it. When it doesn't prove to, he curses the tree, even though the text states that "it was not the season for figs." Although the gospel says that he cursed the tree, I believe he just said something like, "Oh, dry up, I'm going to teach everyone a lesson." Jesus went on to chase the money changers from the Temple, and the following morning when he returned to where the fig tree was, his disciples noticed that it had withered to its roots.

"Look, Master," Peter says, "the fig tree that you doomed the other day has withered." In most translations, Jesus replies to Peter, "Have faith in God," but the original says, "Have the faith of God." That makes a big difference. Jesus then goes on to say, "I tell you if anyone says to this mountain, 'Be lifted up and thrown into the sea,' and does not doubt that what he says will come to be, then that mountain will be tossed into the sea." What Jesus means is that if your thoughts and your emotions are aligned with a sense of congruency, "miracles" will occur.

When the rainmaker in Carl Jung's story prayed, and when Elijah prayed, they did not pray *for* rain. In my estimation, they prayed the word "rain" *with feeling* as a decree. I want to be sure you understand what I mean by the phrase "with feeling," because for some people, it may have overtones of the kind of bad acting known as emoting. I don't mean that at all.

When I was just beginning my healing ministry, I would start every healing service by praying or singing until I began to feel joy and jubilation welling up within me. At that moment, I knew that the healings would begin to flow from the Spirit, and not before. That was the feeling I needed (and still need) to start to call out healings. And it works for me even if it's someone else's service. One time before I began a healing service in New York City, I went to the Times Square Church of Dave Wilkerson, whose congregation is predominantly African American, and I let myself be carried away by the exuberant gospel singing. By the time the service was over, I was so filled with the Spirit that I was in touch with the feeling I needed to carry on a healing service. (The same is true of certain other congregations, such as the parent church of the late John Wimber in Anaheim Hills, California; or Michael Beckwith's Church of Religious Science in Los Angeles.)

If you keep in mind the kind of genuine but soul-stirring feeling I'm talking about here, you'll have some idea what I mean by praying "with feeling." In the case of praying for rain, in this instance, you would remember what it feels like to walk in the rain. Remember how refreshed and filled with tingling excitement you were the last time you witnessed a sunshower, or how awed you were by the sights and sounds of a thunderstorm.

When you pray with feeling like that, you're decreeing that you know something is going to happen. It may happen instantly, it may take an hour, it may be two weeks, but it *will* happen. Sometime ago, I saw that this was the key to effective healing prayer. I realized that the people who truly were in tune with the Divine and were aware of it at the center of their being could begin to pray this way and results would be forthcoming.

You may wonder if you can make a decree by an act of will, or if it is something already revealed to you and you just speak it. My administrative assistant, Bruce, was preparing to fly to Phoenix from Peoria, Illinois, about 150 miles west of

Chicago, for one of my weekend intensives. Other partici-
pants leaving from O'Hare airport in Chicago for that same
weekend didn't get to Arizona until Saturday because a
snowstorm that swept the Chicago area caused delays at the
airport. But when Bruce was praying on Thursday morning
prior to leaving for the airport, he had the distinct thought
that everything was going to be all right for him, and that he
would leave on time. And so he decreed, "Fair weather."
That's what he had—and he left on the same day as the others who arrived late. I believe that much the same thing happened for Elijah, Jesus, and everyone else who decreed in the
Bible. They tapped in to the knowledge and wisdom of God,
they heard the voice of God say something was going to happen, and then they decreed it.

One night many years ago, I went to see Agnes Sanford,
the great healer, who was leading a conference on prayer and
healing in Southern California. The area had been suffering
from a long drought, and no rain was in sight. Before I went
into the meeting, I had heard the TV weatherman bemoan-
ing the fact that there appeared to be no chance of rain over
the next few days. That night, Agnes came out on stage in
front of 3,000 people and said, "I'm sick and tired of hearing
this. Every one of you tells me you are on the spiritual path,
and you complain about the fact that it isn't raining. All right,
now take a lesson."

She looked up, pointed at the ceiling of the building we
were in, and said, "I declare that the rains are now coming
from Southern Mexico." She started naming cloud formations
that were going to come up the Baja Peninsula, sweep over
Anaheim, and pour down on us. She went on like that for
about ten minutes and then she said, "Amen. Now let's get
on with the work for tonight." And she went ahead with her
talk about living the spiritual life.

Before I went to bed that night at the hotel, I turned on
the news, and the same weatherman I had seen earlier came

on at the end. "I can't explain this," he said, "but winds have started coming up from Southern Mexico over the Baja Peninsula, and now they're sweeping into Orange County." He described exactly what Agnes Sanford had said in front of the audience just a few hours before. But the best was yet to come. It started to rain, and the next morning it was still raining. I had made plans to go to Disneyland as soon as the conference was over, so now the downpour that had so delighted me the night before was starting to worry me. If it didn't let up soon, I could forget about Disneyland. I'm sure other people had similar thoughts, because during that day's seminar, we were all looking out the window at the relentless storm, but Agnes didn't pay any attention. Finally, a minister from Southern California raised his hand, which is something Agnes was never wild about.

"Do you have a question?" she asked.

"Yes," he said. "You know the rains are here, just as you said. But I think we've had enough."

Agnes put her hands on her hips and waited for him to finish.

"In all humility," he said, "I'm asking you, can you stop it just like you started it?"

"No," she said. "I gave you awareness of your power. *You* stop it."

Apparently, no one had the power, because for the next four days, it kept raining, and I never did get to Disneyland. When I returned to Illinois, I couldn't get the events of that weekend out of my mind. I was operating a house of prayer at the time and giving workshops on prayer and abundance, telling people how God wants us to live from the spiritual viewpoint, but I was about to learn how to live by the principles I was teaching. For one workshop, we had a lot of last-minute registrations, which came in after I'd already ordered all the food for the evening. I was wondering how we were going to feed them all, so I ran down to the kitchen and started worrying out loud.

A woman from the University of Illinois named Bessie, who was working in the kitchen that night, saw my agitated state and asked calmly, "What's your problem?"

"We have all of these people here, and I don't know how we're going to feed them."

"Aren't you giving a workshop on prayer?" she asked. Before I could answer, she continued, "Well, go do it, and we'll take care of the food."

"Do you have time to go to the store?"

"No," she said. "We'll just pray that it multiplies, so that's no problem."

"What?"

"We'll pray that the food multiplies."

I went upstairs and gave the lecture. During the break, I couldn't help running back down to check on the kitchen again. "Is anybody going to the store?"

Bessie was getting exasperated now. "That's it," she said. "We're going to pray right now. Come over here. Let's form a circle and hold hands."

Bessie led the prayer, and it couldn't have been simpler. "Lord, we have 70 people here, and we made enough food for 30. Multiply the food."

I thought, *This should be part of my lecture upstairs.*

"Amen," she said. "Now go back and do your work." And with that, she left me. At lunch, there was enough food for everyone to have second helpings, and more left for me to take back to the rectory. All of them swore that they hadn't gone out for food, and I believed them.

But the most important point of this story is that the ability to decree is not just a gift. It's a skill that can be developed. Like intuition, we're all born with it, but it takes work to learn to use it. And even those people who have a little more natural ability have to work to get results.

You sometimes hear great basketball stars say that the

most gifted player they ever saw wasn't Michael Jordan or Wilt Chamberlain, but some guy who used to dazzle everyone at a playground court in their neighborhood. The difference between that guy and Jordan was *work*.

As naturally talented as Michael Jordan was, he had to work at it every day. The guy with more natural talent either didn't have the will to work hard, or the discipline to avoid the pitfalls of drugs and other distractions that kept him from developing into a great player. And the same is true of our spiritual skills, whether prayer and meditation, or blessing and decree.

### EXERCISE: DEVELOPING THE SKILL OF DECREE

I learned to develop the skill of decree many years ago by using sacred writings as a foundation of truth upon which to establish my spiritual consciousness. I drew on sections of the Hebrew and Christian Testaments that had special meaning for me, and prayed that truth back to God in the form of affirmation and decree. A couple of simple examples may help you get a sense of how to create your own decrees based on Scripture.

### Decree for Conquering Fear

Let's begin with a line from Psalm 91: "Though a thousand fall on my right, ten thousand on my left, no harm will come to me for I dwell in the presence of the most high God."

I then expand it by affirming: "I do believe I dwell in the secret place of the most high God. I remain grounded in the presence of the almighty God, whose loving power none can withstand. I believe God's Spirit dwells in me.

Because of this, I am without fear or anxiety. The Holy Spirit, who dwells in me, is my strength, and I confidently put my trust in this strength. And so I am not afraid, because God is with me. Because of this, I am grateful. Thank you, God, our Father/Mother, for loving us so much."

### Decree to Overcome Loneliness

This decree is based on Paul's Letter to the Hebrews 13:5-6. (I use the translation in the Amplified Bible, which expands the literal text, with material in brackets):

*. . . for He (God) Himself has said, I will not in any way fail you nor give you up nor leave you without support. [I will] not, [I will] not, [I will] not in any degree leave you helpless, nor forsake nor let [you] down, [relax My hold on you]—assuredly not! So we take comfort and are encouraged and confidently and boldly say,*
   *"The Lord is my Helper,*
   *I will not be seized with alarm—*
   *I will not fear or dread or be terrified."*

After reading that, I say: "With these words, I take comfort and am encouraged. With these words, I know that I am not alone. And for this I am grateful. Thank you, God."

## EXERCISE: DECREE AND THE 23RD PSALM

Now that you're ready for a somewhat longer practice, I want to assure you that no matter what your background, your programming, or religious tradition, each of you can get to a place in life where you can desire and decree. You can have the confidence, power, and authority of the Psalmist in Psalm 23 to know that you are loved by God. But please remind yourself that this won't happen overnight. You may get immediate results at some point in your life, but unless you practice the discipline, I can assure you that the power and authority that is always there will begin to diminish. It's this discipline that keeps feeding your energy, and which brings you to a point where you know, like the Psalmist, that the Lord is your shepherd. There is nothing you lack. It has already been provided. But it *does* take work.

So as you practice this discipline using Psalm 23, you will learn for yourself what prayer is, who the Holy Spirit is, and what kind of energy you're dealing with. You will learn how to heal your life. You come to this awareness as the Psalmist did—by amplifying in your own words the affirmations of this famous prayer of confidence in the Divine:

"The Lord is my shepherd, I shall not want." There isn't a thing I need but is already provided.

"He makes me lie down in green pastures." When I relax, I listen and I connect. I hear the voice guide me and direct me because it is the shepherd's voice.

"He leads me beside the peaceful waters." Then as I hear that voice, I'm guided by that voice. That's how God refreshes and restores my very being. He leads me in the path of right thinking, right action, right speaking, right doing, right being for the glory of His name.

"Though I walk through the valley of the shadow"—that is, the illusion—"of death, I will fear nor dread no error or evil, for God is with me."

"Thy rod and thy staff they comfort me." The rod and staff in Scripture are the symbols of power and authority, respectively. Today the word *comfort* usually denotes creature comforts—a big leather armchair in front of a large-screen TV. But our word *comfort* comes from the Latin *confortare*, which means "to strengthen greatly, to empower." The Holy Spirit, by Her very presence, empowers us.

"You strengthen me, and in the presence of my enemies, you anoint my head with oil. My cup runneth over." Enemies can refer not only to outer but also to inner enemies—the ego, fear, neuroses. You make me aware of the oil of the Divine Spirit. Therefore, my cup of living brims over.

"Surely now I know only goodness and mercy and unfailing love will follow me all the days of my life, for I dwell in the house of the Lord." The house is the Spirit, the energy, the consciousness of the Divine presence. Those words are comforting in themselves.

### The Principles Work . . . If You Work the Principles

After a workshop I was giving, a woman came up to me and said, "I enjoyed the information you gave, but you really pressed my button."

"What do you mean by that?" I asked.

"When you mentioned God," she explained. "I don't like to use that name."

*Then use another one,* I thought. *What's the big deal?* What I said was, "That's right. I might have pressed that button, but the button belongs entirely to you. Do something about it."

I learned a long time ago that one of the quickest ways to get people's attention is to interrupt their thought patterns. Those thought patterns are what we use to make excuses for what's happening in our lives. We want to point the finger at something outside of ourselves, when all we really need to do is practice meditation or prayer and take a good look within. Whenever you think or feel something, you're making a choice, consciously or unconsciously, for either life or death, and that's what's going to activate the body processes within you.

If you study the prayer habits of the ancient mystics, you'll discover that they include body movement. Along with kneeling and sitting and the lotus posture, these body movements may involve bowing or prostration—spreading the body out in a full face-down posture on the floor—all of which activate a specific vibration. Kneeling, for example, is a sign of humility to most people, a receptivity to accept something from a higher power, just as bowing before the king or queen in earlier cultures indicated submission to their will. Some people get profound inspirations just from sitting in a chair, as we do during my healing services. If during prayer or a healing service you feel the need to stand or kneel, you should follow that impulse, because in the process of doing so, you're activating healing energy more powerfully from within your being.

In the sacred literature of the world, especially the Christian literature, we can read the accounts of the Holy Spirit descending upon various mystics. But the 13th-century mystic Meister Eckhart made the point that the Holy Spirit isn't so much *descending* on us as *coming forth* from within us and through us. When we talk about this Divine energy—whatever name we give it—we should understand that it's also coming from within our being, because we are the energy of God. The early Christian mystics recognized that each of us is a spark of God, or what they termed *the holy Monad*.[1] We have that spark of God, even if we don't yet know it—and even if the flicker of that flame is all but going out.

In the East, they refer to this Divine energy as *prana* or *chi*, the enlivening force that flows throughout the body. The guiding principle behind Hatha Yoga and acupuncture is to unblock the inner pathways of the body—either through psychophysical exercises or through the use of needles or pressure applied to certain crucial points along the inner meridians—and facilitate the flow of this great Divine energy.

After his enlightenment, the Buddha did not acknowledge a Supreme Being because he wanted us to understand that we have the source of enlightenment within us. Many people think of Buddhism as an atheistic religion, but the

Buddha actually did accept the existence of the gods of the Hindu pantheon of his day. He reportedly visited the god realms during his enlightenment, but he said that the deities were not essentially better off than humans because they weren't motivated to seek enlightenment as we are. Having been raised in the Jewish or Christian tradition, Westerners may not agree with the Buddha's rejection of a Supreme Being, but we should at least learn to embrace the notion that Divinity begins within each of us.

ᏈᎧᏋ

When I studied how the ancients prayed, I found that they experienced emotions physically. I realized just how true this was when I thought back to an incident from my youth.

Most of us have had at least one experience of a broken relationship, and I was no exception. My most memorable one came when I was in junior college (equivalent to today's two-year community college). I was going out with a woman who was also a student, and I was certain that we were going to get married. (I later learned the truth in the old saying that if you want to see God laugh, tell Him your plans.)

This girl and I even had a favorite song, Ivory Joe Hunter's "Since I Met You, Baby." Whenever we went somewhere, we would press the band to play that. Yet, after a year or so, I no longer found that the relationship was sustaining me or maintaining my joy. But I put off acknowledging this to her for eight or nine months because I didn't want to hurt her feelings. All the while, I was getting crabbier and more resentful, to the point where I was shouting at her. I had bought into the idea that it was better to stay together and not hurt my girlfriend's feelings, even if it meant brutalizing her emotionally because I was doing something I no longer wanted to do. I was probably hoping that she'd get sick of me and break up with me.

One night at a school dance, I decided that the time was finally right for me to tell her. I was going to wait until we were on that dance floor and then I would say, "Honey, I really loved our time together. I really loved it, but it's over." Between songs, I was trying to decide the most tactful way to phrase it. We did a lot of dancing that night before I was able to work up the courage. I was finally ready to tell her when she turned to me and said, "I've got a surprise for you."

"Oh, what's that?" I asked.

"Listen to the band," she said, and, of course, they began to play "Since I Met You Baby." As we started dancing to it, she said, "Now, you had something to tell me?"

"Yes, I do." And conscious of the supreme irony of the music that was playing, I went through with my plan and told her how I felt. She took it very well, which surprised me. Our parents, on the other hand, did not take it well at all. The tribe was extremely upset. The gal was Polish, and my mother, who was also Polish, had visualized a glorious Polish wedding in our future. My girlfriend's mother had visualized the same thing, but it never did take place. The upshot was extremely painful and messy all around, and was much worse than it would have been if I had announced my feelings a year before.

I thought I had dealt with it, however, and went on years later to become a Catholic priest. One day I was listening to one of those stations that plays all the Golden Oldies when the deejay announced that he was going to play another favorite from the '50s. He announced, "I hope you enjoy it. Here's Ivory Joe Hunter with 'Since I Met You Baby.'" I felt as if someone had punched me in the stomach. All of the emotions of 20 years ago were still present in me, and I clearly hadn't dealt with them as well as I'd thought.

As I've already said, when "healing the memories," we don't get rid of the memory, but we do get rid of the negative sting that accompanies the memory. That negative energy is still locked in your body, and that's what you feel when the memory is evoked. You may respond by getting a headache, restlessness, shortness of breath, and/or a constricted feeling in the pit of the stomach or in the heart region, as happened with me on that occasion. It's all an indication that something at the center of your being is not yet at peace.

The ancients understood this principle that the body is a tremendous vehicle to experience the voice and presence of God, and they incorporated that knowledge into their prayers. When I studied the prayer life of the Essenes, the ascetical sect who practiced in the area around the Dead Sea during the time of Christ, I found that when they meditated, they would look at the three components of their life: thoughts, feelings, and the body.

For instance, when you're not peaceful, your body vibrates with restlessness. We can say that God is love, but we have so many definitions for love today that it's hard to have a direct emotional or physical correlation for that love. But when we bring the word *peace* into our consciousness, our bodies immediately let us know whether we have peace or not. The Essenes would invoke the word *peace,* by which they meant "the presence of God," and they would begin their prayer time by saying repeatedly, "Peace to my thoughts, peace to my body, peace to my feelings."

What the Essenes were doing was decreeing peace within themselves. They were not *asking* for peace to come; they were *declaring* it. They were saying that peace is already here, and they just need to be aware of it.

One time after I had led a healing celebration while still a priest, I went into the back room to take off my vestments. As I turned sideways, I saw what looked like a head of hair the size of Marge Simpson's come through the doorway—this was in the days when women used to wear towering beehive hairdos. The woman stood straight up and said, "You know, Father, I have a gift just like you." I asked her to explain what it was and she said, "I'm able to read people's faults and then tell them all about it."

At that moment, all of the Christ nature drained from my being and I wanted to throttle her. When people start telling you what special powers they have, they're not truly secure in their authority. Today, plenty of books are being written about reclaiming your power, but it does no good to reclaim your power if you don't know that you have the authority to use it. It's like looking at a roast turkey sitting on the table and saying, "Lord, that looks good. I wonder what it would taste like. I haven't eaten a good meal for months, and that looks like the most delicious thing I've ever seen." And as you're admiring the turkey, instead of eating it, you die of starvation. That's the way it is with power. Everybody has the spiritual power, but not everybody knows that they have the authority to use it. That's what made mystics like the Essenes different: They *knew* they had the authority, and they would decree something to happen.

The Book of Job says, "Thou shalt decree a thing and it shall come to pass." But in order for you to decree it to come to pass, using faith as the energy to command, you must experience a sense of tranquility in your thoughts, your feelings, and your body. If your body is anxious, your thoughts and feelings will be that way. Since all emotions spring from either love or fear, if you bring love to your body, you cannot fear anything. So begin by saying, "Love to my body. Love to my body. Love to my body." Because our thoughts are so scattered, you continue your meditation by saying, "Peace to my thoughts. Peace to my thoughts. Peace to my thoughts." You can have the right thoughts and the right physical sensations, but if you're feeling that "I probably won't get it" or "God, it feels awful to be sick," then that has to be changed. The best way to do this is to bring the word *joy* into your feelings by repeating, "Joy to my feelings. Joy to my feelings. Joy to my feelings." So you're saying "Peace to my thoughts. Love to my body. Joy to my feelings."

When you do this long enough—it may be days, or months, or a year—something will click, and when it does, you'll know that you're now at the point of decreeing.

John of the Cross likened the soul to a ship that sits at a dock. When a ship is moored at a dock, it doesn't go anywhere, but barnacles and grime attach themselves to the hull. If you want the boat to operate harmoniously in a state of balance, you have to clean off the barnacles and grime and then send it out on the water. John was saying, in effect, "As you move through life, you gather up all these barnacles—resentment, bitterness, unforgiveness, anger, and envy. You have to come to a point where you invite the spirit of God to help you transform those barnacles. That can only lead to a sense of enlightenment, meaning that you're becoming aware of the light at the center of your being."

The dark night of the soul that he described so eloquently is essential to our development, because within that darkness is light. We travel through the tunnel of darkness to get to the light. Once that happens, you move into the stage of healing called *Divine union*, in which you know that you are one with God. You don't "believe" it, because every belief is filled with doubts. Instead, you *know* it with every fiber of your being, and nothing and no one can sever you from that oneness. At that point, the decree starts coming, and your prayer life begins to change.

### Decreeing Health

When you decree health, something begins to happen. You have more stamina in your body; you don't know what's going on, but you do know that when you wake up, you feel different because something is going on deep within. You've learned that if you are one with God, then everything God has potentially belongs to you. If that's true, you can begin to decree things simply by saying what God said when He created the universe: "Let there be. . . ."

In the Book of Genesis, the first thing God creates is light. But He doesn't create the sun, moon, and stars until later. We now know from science that everything in creation *is* light. As wonderful as this body of matter that we live within may seem to us, and as astonishing as it actually is once we begin to understand its extraordinary complexity and its ability to regenerate itself, it's still not who I am. I am light. And if I am light, I can travel anywhere, which is the simple explanation for the apparently illogical fact that some mystics can bilocate, or appear in two places at once. If we are light, and light travels at a speed of 132,000 miles per second, what's the problem with being in Italy one moment and Peru the next? The Orthodox Christians refer to the fifth stage of enlightenment or healing as *deification*. You recognize that you are a part of God, and that at the center of your being is the Divine, so when you say, "Let there be," you genuinely expect something to happen.

Ask yourself how you are praying right now. Are you praying for something? Because if you *are* praying for something, you are literally saying, "I don't have it." If you're praying for health, you're saying, "I don't have health, and I won't get it without begging for it." So the more you keep praying that way, the more your focus is on lack. Even if it's uncomfortable for you, begin to pray "health," begin to pray "healthy relationships," begin to pray "abundance," in such a way that you're decreeing it with feeling. Again, praying or decreeing "with feeling" means to recall a time, perhaps as a child, when you were able to enjoy perfect health. Or remember what a healthy relationship felt like, when there was someone in your life with whom you were truly close, maybe a parent, sibling, dear friend, or relative.

As the old saying goes, sometimes you have to fake it until

you make it. You may say to yourself, *Gee, I've been saying this stuff, and I don't know if it's working*. That is the problem with saying affirmations alone. When many people make affirmations, they aren't completely convinced that they'll work, so they don't. The affirmations must be *decrees said with feeling*, which is to say that they must come from a heart that knows, "When I say it, it's going to be done, and if I'm saying it for another person, it can only be done to the extent of their receptivity."

### The Healing Touch from Within

Some people cling to the notion that a person—me or somebody like me—who is graced with healing ability needs to touch them and work with them individually for them to be healed. You don't need me or anyone else to touch you; you only need God to touch you. That can happen anywhere at any time. My role is to show you how to get into that atmosphere so it can happen.

When I was leading a healing service for a couple of hundred people in Indianapolis a few years ago, I called a woman up to the platform who was going through a lot of trauma over her encroaching deafness. Within five minutes, she could hear, and she left her hearing aids behind. After lunch that day, a gentleman came up and asked if he could talk to me. He told me that during the service he had felt something in his body, yet his mind didn't want to believe what had happened. I asked him to explain.

He told me, "I came here with two hearing aids, just like the woman you worked with this morning," adding that he had been sitting in the last row. "When you were working with her, though, they started making such a terrible electric noise that I took them out. And when I did, I could hear everything you said, even when you turned the microphone off as you were testing her ears." Four months after that, I saw him again. He had received a clean bill of health from his medical doctors, who admitted that they didn't know what had happened.

One especially dramatic yet mystifying form of healing within occurs when someone goes down "under the power," usually falling backward or crumpling to the ground after being touched on the forehead during a healing service. The best way I can explain what happens at that moment is that the healing current is being released for that individual. It doesn't happen to everyone, because the people who truly go under have short-circuited their bodies. I believe the body is created with a specific vibration and frequency, and when the Spirit of God enters the picture with a higher voltage and higher frequency, we can literally pass out from the shock.

During the 30 years I've witnessed this phenomenon, I haven't come up with a better explanation. In almost every case that I've followed up on, the people who went down and remained under for perhaps 15 to 30 minutes were healed of deep emotional traumas, often on an unconscious level. They could not face the trauma consciously at this point in life, yet their commitment to get on with their life was so strong that the Divine answered their prayer. Somehow that energy moved through them and healed them, and when the memory came back, either later that day or many days or even years afterward, the sting wasn't there anymore. That's quick high-voltage work, but it has nothing to do with me. I simply facilitate the healing and do what I am told intuitively.

A woman who was healed at one of my services came to the microphone and said, "It took a lot of faith for me to come up here, because I told somebody at lunch that I believed everybody else could be healed but me." This, unfortunately, is the mind-set of many people. Those who take my five-day intensive healing prayer workshops often say, "I would have come up to be healed, but so-and-so needed it more." They think it's selfish to claim something for themselves. I tell them, "Why don't you begin to see it as sanctified selfishness?" What they are actually saying in their consciousness is, "I don't deserve this because I'm no good. I'm a worm." But everybody deserves this. If you had ten children who were sick, you wouldn't pick one and say, "Honey, the other nine deserve to get well, but I'm afraid you don't." Yet that's the image we have of God. When we get sick, we believe that God has brought it upon us. Worse than that, clergy who go visiting the sick often tell them, "You're sick because God loves you more. Your suffering is pleasing to God."

A woman in my parish once told me that she learned a lesson quite young in life when her seven-year-old boy fell off his bicycle, scraped his knees, and ran in crying and screaming, "Ma, help me! It hurts!" Trying to be a good mother and soothe her child, the woman put her arm around the boy and said, as a good Catholic, "Tommy, I want you to quit crying and offer it up to God."

In an instant, she told me, he looked at her and said, "Are you nuts? If I don't want this pain, what makes you think He wants it?"

Tommy spoke with the unalloyed directness of youth. Pain can certainly be a great teacher, but we shouldn't consider it an end in itself. If pain is such a good thing, as some recent self-help books suggest, why don't we ever hear Jesus in the Gospels suggesting that people hold on to their pain rather than be healed? He doesn't tell the paralytic, "Go home and suffer a little more, and then come back and see me in two weeks."

When loving parents see their children in pain, they immediately try to alleviate their suffering—and the same is true of God. Yet I acknowledge that pain can play an important role in our lives, which is one reason why I don't necessarily advocate quick fixes whenever we feel pain. It's there to teach us to deal with the underlying problem before the situation gets worse. One of the most insidious diseases on earth, although it is extremely rare, renders people impervious to pain. Children who suffer from Hereditary Sensory and Autonomic Neuropathy can literally walk around with a broken bone and not know it.

That might sound attractive until you consider the consequences. When you feel a pain in your tooth, for example, the pain isn't there to ennoble you. It's there to tell you to get to the dentist and treat the underlying condition—perhaps to get a crown, or a root canal. If you don't do something about it soon, you'll probably end up losing that tooth and maybe a few more, just as carrying on with your life with a broken arm can eventually lead to losing the use of that limb, and perhaps worse.

So when you have a pain, sit up and take notice of it. Then ask the Spirit what the reason is for this pain. Listen carefully for an answer, which will represent the wisdom from within. Even if you don't get an answer to what's causing the pain, you may get a simple answer to go to the doctor, the chiropractor, the holistic healer, or to change your diet or some aspect of your lifestyle. I would advise you to follow that direction, because it represents yet another manifestation of the healing touch from within. It isn't always an immediate cure, but the still, small voice that speaks to us can direct us onto the path that will eventually lead to a cure or a healing.

Just after he turned 71, the great 20th-century healer Smith Wigglesworth suffered a painful attack of kidney stones. Although his physician warned him that unless he had surgery he would die, Wigglesworth insisted that "the God who made this body is the One who can cure it. No knife shall ever cut it as long as I live." He respected his inner voice and continued to suffer with the kidney stones for six long years, but in time, the condition was healed from within. Over that time, Wigglesworth passed more than 100 stones naturally, often having to interrupt a service to withdraw and minister to himself. Yet he never had a major illness after that, and he lived a productive life into his late 80s.

---

[1] For further discussion of the Monad, see Kyriacos Markides, *The Magus of Stravolus* and *Homage to the Sun: The Wisdom of the Magus of Stravolus.*

# Chapter Three

⟨ornament⟩

# The Heart of Matter

What I wish for you to learn most of all is how to relinquish the control of your life to the Divine Essence that each of you are. That means, as Caroline Myss likes to say, being an "elegant spirit," living consciously, developing skills of awareness and insight that release you from having to feel victimized or controlled ever again by life's challenges. I regard this quality of spiritual power as the force that transforms us in such a way that we move through life with elegance and grace. An elegant spirit is one who practices unconditional love, an attitude of nonjudgment, and who lives in the spirit of wisdom and compassion—allowing others to feel safe in his or her presence. An elegant spirit does not denigrate matter, but rather, appreciates all matter as being created by God.

To be an elegant spirit, you must learn to love matter, to respect matter, yet you must also come to the point where matter no longer controls you. While you're in this body, then, *enjoy* the body. When I talk about healing and the role of prayer, I'm talking from a holistic viewpoint, meaning that the Spirit of God can move and heal and restore you instantly. But then *your* responsibility is to take care of your thought patterns. It's up to you to eat properly, exercise, and take care of yourself and maintain that joy that's part of being free.

On the level of spiritual traditions, my teacher is Jesus. But

I assure you that it doesn't matter to God whatever your path is. I want to show you how each of us can follow the path we are on and live what our teacher tells us to live. There isn't a major religion in the world today that doesn't have at its foundation unconditional love. It's about time we all accept that challenge and start practicing it. When I quote Scripture, most times it will be from the Christian Testament or the Hebrew Testament, because I know them better than I know the *Bhagavad Gita* or the Quran. But surely the principles are the same. I have discovered in 30 years of work that whether you follow the Muslim path, the Jewish path, the Hindu path, the Native American path, the Buddhist path, or the Christian path, it's up to you to take those principles and apply them. Every one of us can live our path in a way that is extremely joyful, healing, reconciling, powerful, and filled with peace.

### Love Is Common to All Religions

Spiritual healing is experiencing God's love on some level of our being. Here is how each of the major world religious traditions expresses the law of love.

**Judaism:** You shall love your neighbor as yourself.

**Christianity:** Do unto others as you would have them do unto you.

**Islam:** No one of you is a believer until he [she] loves for his brother [sister] what he [she] loves for himself [herself].

**Hinduism:** People gifted with intelligence should always treat others as they themselves wish to be treated.

**Buddhism:** In five ways should a clansman minister to friends and familiars: generosity, courtesy, and benevolence, by treating them as he treats himself, and by being as good as his word.

**Taoism:** Regard your neighbor's gain as your own gain, and regard your neighbor's love as your own.

**Confucianism:** What you do not want done to yourself, do not do to others.

∽ৎ

My philosophy is not either/or, but rather both/and. Just as I don't believe you have to belittle Buddhism to be a Christian, neither do I think that you have to abandon medicine to try prayer—or ignore prayer to use psychology. Use everything at your disposal. The key is changing our paradigm, or worldview. That requires seeing the world not only with our physical eyes, but also with the eyes of our spirit. It means using not only one hemisphere of the brain, but both simultaneously—that is, not logic *or* creativity, but logic *and* creativity.

Healing isn't just about your body or someone else's body. It's about mind and will. It's about careers, relationships—whatever it is that makes us whole human beings. I try to make a fine distinction between healing and curing. Healing is still a process, although faster than what has traditionally been the medical process.

Say, for example, you break your arm or leg and you have it x-rayed and put in a cast, and you've been told by the best medical minds that it will be eight weeks before the cast comes off. So you call in friends who see God or the Divine energy as love, as desiring to help and not condemn. They can come and lay hands on the cast and they pray, or maybe just get still and meditate. Maybe they sing some songs. I call that God's radiation therapy. Then you go back for a checkup and the doctor doesn't understand it. In two weeks, the bone is totally healed. That's still a process; it wasn't instantaneous.

A cure, on the other hand, is something that happens instantaneously. I once heard Dr. Bernie Siegel talk about remission. He said that doctors often don't know what has happened, so they tell you that your disease has "gone into remission." According to Dr. Siegel, that's just a nice phrase meaning "Damned if I know what happened."

When I work with people, I pray three words: COME, HOLY SPIRIT. I'm calling forth that Divine Essence at the center of their being to come forth and restore them.

### EXERCISE: BREATHING

The universal technique for meditation is breathing. All spiritual paths teach breathing as the first exercise in praying and extending one's consciousness in the awareness of the Divine Connection. You bring the breath through your nose all the way down through your diaphragm, so that on the inhale your stomach extends outward, and on the exhale the diaphragm area comes back in. Then close your eyes and take another deep breath. Inhale. Hold it for a second or two, and then exhale. Then do it again. Just continue to breathe normally. When I ask you to take a deep breath, I don't want you to try to focus or concentrate. I want you only to be aware. Just be aware of the breath passing through your nostrils. Follow it going down into the diaphragm, and then be aware of the breath coming out through your nostrils. It may help you to place the palms of your hands on your belly as you breathe and feel them expand outward as you breathe in, and return to their initial position as you exhale.

Breathing is important to relaxation because even after most people get up in the morning and attempt to pray or meditate, they're still stressed out from the night before. If you watch TV prior to going to bed, especially any type of negative programming, including the news, that can produce a lot of stress and negative energy that you bring into sleep. The result can be powerfully negative dreams or nightmares, and so when you wake up in the morning, you feel anything but peaceful. A good sign of your restlessness is that when you begin this particular exercise, you may start coughing. In all likelihood, that means that you have been shortening your breath, which is the way most of us breathe all day long—taking short, shallow breaths like rabbits. These short breaths don't activate the calming receptors located in the lower lobes of the lungs. Rather, they keep us in a constant state of excitation. Think of how you breathe when you're frightened, say, when you have to dodge out of the way of a speeding car or truck. Your breath and pulse have speeded up—which is good in that instance, because you need to move fast to survive. But if you keep breathing that way all day long, you'll wear yourself out.

When you begin this practice, especially if you haven't had much experience in deep breathing, your lungs and neck may begin to constrict. They have difficulty adapting to this more intense way of breathing and can't take in so much air; that's a good indication that you're stressed out. Do not focus. Do not concentrate. Just be aware. Inhale. Hold it. Exhale. Inhale. Hold it. Exhale. Inhale. Hold it. Continue to breathe normally.

Now I want you to bring into consciousness the words I AM. On the exhale, bring into your consciousness the words GOD BREATHED. Now, combine them on the inhale and exhale: I AM GOD BREATHED. Be aware of any pain in your body, any tension, stress, or anxious thoughts. Don't try to fight them. Just bring into your consciousness on the inhale the word PEACE, and on the exhale the same thing: PEACE. Continue to breathe normally. Next bring in the word LOVE on the inhale and LOVE on the exhale. Be aware of the breath moving through your body, and continue to breathe normally.

Finally, bring the word FREEDOM into your consciousness when you inhale and exhale. Take a deep breath and inhale, exhale, inhale, exhale, inhale, exhale. Continue to breathe normally. Now enter the silence.

∽♪∾

You've just had a little taste of what prayer was to the ancients, whether they were Christian, Jewish, Hindu, Buddhist, Taoist, or Muslim. Real prayer is from the heart, which, as you may have noticed, is in the center of your body. It's not in your head, or in your eyes, or in your mind's eye. The books about Eastern Orthodox Christianity often speak of the form called the Prayer of the Heart, but to all genuine mystics, there is only one form of prayer, and it's expressed in the heart.

## Turning Life Rightside Up by Surrendering

The Tao Te Ching says:

*Always we hope someone else has the answer.*
*Some other place will be better*
*Some other time it will all turn out.*
*This is it.*
*No one else has the answer*
*No other place will be better*
*And it has already turned out.*
*At the center of your Being you have the answer.*

*You know who you are.*
*And you know what you want.*
*There is no need to run outside for better seeing.*
*Nor to peer from a window. Rather*
*Abide at the center of your Being.*
*For the more you leave it the less you learn.*
*Search your heart and see*
*The way to DO is to BE.*

That particular reflection recapitulates in its own way most of the teachings about the dark night of the soul. As originally conceived by the 16th-century Spanish mystic St. John of the Cross, who coined the phrase, the dark night of the soul was "the dark night of enlightenment." In *Prayer and the Five Stages of Healing*, I explained that this makes up the fourth stage of healing or spiritual enlightenment. What makes this stage so powerful compared to the three earlier stages known as the awakening, the purification, and the illumination, is that during this stage, the Divine enters the picture. By that I mean that the Divine takes you at your word that you want enlightenment, and turns your life rightside up.

Whenever I make that statement at a workshop, someone usually says, "You mean God turns it upside down." I have to explain that our life is already that way—we just haven't become aware of it. All the confusion we feel—all the despair, depression, anxiety, and worry—are indications that our life is already in a state of chaotic turmoil. No matter where we look in our life, we find dysfunction. If we contemplate our material status, we may see that we're successful, yet we're also in a state of confusion, anxiety, worry, and continual stress. We're concerned that our success may end, that our material possessions may be taken away from us, and that our life is not really a success. To make life successful, we need relationships. Whether you go to a church, temple, mosque, synagogue, or other religious organization, you stay for only one reason—relationships. The great commandment, as Jesus expounded it, is about having a relationship with the Divine, with yourself, and with others.

When you become genuinely committed to the spiritual path, God perks up and gives a big whistle, and one million angels come. Then He says, "Did you hear that? Let's see if this one really meant it." Suddenly, things begin to happen in your life that appear to be disastrous and negative but are actually leading you closer to the Divine. That's why the Master Jesus said we are never to judge by appearances. You have to convince yourself that you're willing to pay the price for staying on the path. When you first get close to the Holy Spirit, you feel Her refreshment. But after the refreshment comes the flame, the same flame that descended on the disciples at the first Pentecost. The flame represents God's purging of everything you hold dear, because God is saying, "I'm number one in your life now, not anything else." When you get that straight, then you begin to live in a very fruitful manner.

The reason for the dark night, as John of the Cross talks about it, is not to release us from material things because we've been abusing them or because they've been leading us away from God. If you're still at that stage of consciousness, you probably won't encounter the dark night at all. The purpose of the dark night is not to remove material things from our life at all, but rather, to release us from those attachments to which we still cling. Indeed, the end toward which that entire experience is moving us can be summed up in one word: *surrender*. The very word has a bad connotation these days, equated as it is with losing the battle or the war and resigning yourself to defeat. But in spiritual terminology, surrender has nothing to do with resignation, which can often be about self-pity. When you're moving through the dark night, you'll get to the point where you finally say, "That's it. I don't know what to do anymore. I surrender." And that's when all the angels start dancing. They act a little like Professor Higgins in *My Fair Lady,* when Eliza Doolittle finds the right accent: "By George, I think she's got it! She's finally got it!"

Medical research has shown that when people battle a serious disease, they sometimes get to the point where they surrender and say, "Okay, that's it. I can't seem to do anything about this disease. It may kill me, but from this point on, I'm living life to the fullest." In those cases, often within a short time, the disease is completely gone.

There is a place in the former Yugoslavia called Medjugorje where the Blessed Mother is said to have appeared over the last 15 years. I've been there four times now, and each time has been a profound experience. One of the priests who has witnessed many of the healings there told me that the people who were healed often came with one thought: *I don't know the will of God in this matter, but I'm going to surrender to it.* Healings don't happen all the time, but more often than not, they *do* happen during the act of surrender. Resignation is not the same as surrender. Resignation—as in being resigned to one's fate—is a passive emotion. Surrender, by contrast, is an active expression of trust. In military terms, one can see surrender as a positive action that prevents more bloodshed and the loss of more lives and resources. The military leader who is either in denial and fights to the death, or is resigned to his eventual defeat but wants to take down with him as many of the enemy as he can, is doomed.

When my father had his first brush with death, I was shocked at the sight. I went into his room and saw him bleeding from the nose and the mouth, with blood all over the walls. My father was an alcoholic, and his liver was starting to give out. None of us knew what to do. My first reaction was to think, *I'm going to pray. God, if this is his time to go, then let him go in peace now. If not, heal him now.*

He was healed instantly, and I thought, *This is great!*

The only problem was that he gave up drinking for about six months and then went back to it. So the next time he had an attack like that, it really *was* time to go, because his liver had disintegrated. In the hospital, you could even see bits of his liver coming through the tube, and he was in a state of what I called "coma vibration." He was in a coma, but his body was shaking up and down without stopping. The doctors tried everything to stop the shaking, but to no avail. I asked if he was conscious, and they said he wasn't. This was before the case studies had come out demonstrating that unconscious patients who were being operated on could hear everything the doctors were saying, yet I intuitively knew this. I said to God that there must be something I could do to stop the awful shaking. And I heard an inner voice telling me, "Yes, just tell it to stop."

I did, very softly but firmly, and that was the end of it. The shaking stopped. As I sat there, I heard the voice say to me, "Now, forgive your father." At first I thought it was the "devil" this time. All I could think was that my father was a bad man who drank too much and yelled at us and made everyone unhappy. How could I forgive him for that? The voice came again: "Forgive him." Finally, I surrendered to it. I stood up over the bed and actually whispered aloud, "Dad, I forgive you."

Immediately, he opened his eyes and looked at me. "And I forgive you," he said. Then he closed his eyes and seemed to return to his coma. I was stunned. My first reaction was, *Oh my God, that's wonderful.* And then I thought, *What do you mean, you forgive me?*

It was close to midnight, and my mother and I were both in the room. Then with all the windows in the hospital closed, we could smell a fragrant aroma of flowers wafting through the room. I went out into the hallway to see who was bringing in flowers. I opened the windows to see if it was coming from outside, but when I stuck my head out, I couldn't smell anything.

My mother said it was time to go. We lived only ten minutes away, yet I knew that by the time we got home, my father would be dead. When we arrived home, the phone was already ringing. It was the nurse telling us to come back because Dad had passed away just after we left. I felt no resentment, however, because I'd had the opportunity for closure. And I was able to reach closure only because I listened to the voice that was telling me, in essence, to surrender by letting go of my bitterness toward my father for being an alcoholic. I don't know where I would have gone psychically or what my life would be right now without having had the chance to forgive him.

If you've never had the opportunity to put closure on something, you can still do it in the world of Spirit. You can still go back to that time by setting the scene again in your mind. If it's someone you never forgave for hurting you, you can go back and do the forgiving and let them forgive you. Remember that none of us is completely guiltless; we've all done things to each other that we need to heal emotionally. Physical healing isn't the only kind. The Spirit of God is very good at emotional healing, too.

What you most need to remember about the dark night is that it's about clinging. After Jesus died and was raised from the dead, according to one Gospel account (John 20:17), he appeared to Mary Magdalene, who at first did not recognize him in his risen form. When she finally realized it was Jesus, he said, "Do not hold me," also translated as "Do not cling to me." That scene became a favorite of artists and is called *noli me tangere*, from the Latin version of the text, which is usually rendered "Do not touch me." But that is not the same thing as "Do not cling to me."

I read Scripture for its historical, metaphorical, and mystical value because I'm looking for an underlying principle. When I first saw the word *cling* in a translation of that verse, I realized that it was a message that I could relate to the later writings of John of the Cross. Material possessions aren't the problem; *clinging* to them is. If we become overly attached to things, we can't surrender. Many of us cling to sickness, either as a way of getting attention or pity, or as a way of preventing ourselves from moving on as we would do if we were healthy. And some of us even cling to health, overcome with fear that we couldn't handle sickness; conversely, if we're sick, we see health as the Holy Grail. What John of the Cross is saying is to beware of these kinds of attachments to the realm of matter.

## EXERCISE: HEART CHAKRA MEDITATION

If you've studied or worked with the seven chakras, or psychospiritual energy centers, this exercise will be very meaningful for you. If you come from another tradition that may not understand chakras, just think of the heart center, the fourth chakra, as the seat of God. Especially in the Roman Catholic or Eastern Orthodox traditions, this imagery may draw you back to the pictures and statues of Jesus and Mary, where their sacred hearts are exposed, often on fire; or St. Jude, with the image of Jesus over his heart. That imagery isn't an accident. Our spiritual DNA is encoded with a belief in the power at the center of our material being. Those sacred drawings were attempts to depict the love of God at the center of our being. And many paintings show Jesus, Mary, the saints, or the apostles with a nimbus of light surrounding their heads. In Eastern terminology, that is the seventh chakra, located just above the crown of the head, which radiates with the bright white light of spiritual realization.

This is a very simple meditation that you can do when you are tense, frustrated, or angry. To be honest, when I get frustrated, I sometimes won't even think of doing it, because for a moment or two, self-pity seems so much more appealing. But when you realize that it only accumulates more negative energy, that's the time to take a deep breath and go into something like this. You can even do it at work. You may not be able to do it at your desk or work station, but you can always make an excuse and go to the bathroom where you're alone for the two or three minutes it takes. When you have the time at home, you can practice this exercise for 10 or 15 minutes. Once you get the hang of it, you can do it in two or three minutes if need be, just long enough to begin to feel the harmony coming back into your being.

Remember how you learned to breathe deeply in the previous exercise. Take a deep breath in through your nose, and let it out slowly through your nose or mouth. Repeat that two more times, then put your head down so that your jaw is resting on your chest and your eyes are gazing at your heart area. Don't try to focus on your physical heart, but rather, on a spot at the very center of your chest about level with your heart. Then bring the breath into your consciousness again, but this time move it from the nose to the heart. As you're breathing, watch your diaphragm expand, and aim your gaze at your heart until you know you're ready to imagine that you're breathing in and out through your heart rather than through your nose. On every inhalation, keep your eyes focused on your heart until you can close your eyes and sense that you're bringing in the breath through your heart.

If you've never done this before, don't get discouraged. You may not be able to do it right off, but in a few days you'll be able to do it quite well. You don't have to take deep breaths; just breathe normally, but if deep breathing feels good to you, then go ahead and do that. When you see the diaphragm rising and descending, your thought is: *I am breathing through my heart.* If you're comfortable and able to do it, you can close your eyes while continuing to recognize that you're breathing through your heart. And then bring in the word *love.* Inhale *love.* Exhale *love.* Then bring in the word *peace,* and do the same with it. You can add other words throughout the day, such as *joy* or *freedom*. You may want to stop five or six times during the day and do this for two or three minutes, using a different word each time. Then close the meditation with the phrase, "I am love. I am love." Now take a deep breath and open your eyes.

When I give these exercises in my workshops, some people complain that meditating like this makes them doze off or fall asleep. If that happens to you, it's likely that your body is telling you that it's too stressed. When you start this form of meditation, there's nothing wrong with falling asleep (just don't try it in the bathtub until you know you can stay awake). But you'd probably better get more sleep or reduce the levels of stress in your life. In time you'll get over it. In some cases, where a great deal of negative energy is present in you, you may go out like a light because that energy doesn't want you to feel this sacred space of meditation. You have to learn to discern when you're falling asleep because your body is telling you that it needs more rest or less stress, and when negative spiritual and psychological energies are working against you.

# Chapter Four

❧❧

## Healing the Body by Healing the Mind and Heart

T hings happen in our lives because we believe in our subconscious mind that they *should* be happening. Yet when something bad happens, like an illness, you may say to yourself, "How can this be? I haven't been sitting here asking to get this disease." But it doesn't work that way. According to Carl Jung, the mind is divided into three parts: the conscious mind; the subconscious; and the superconscious, where the Spirit of God dwells. For the purpose of inner healing, we will talk mainly about the conscious and subconscious mind. Your conscious mind is the thinking mind, the part of you that stands in front of the mirror in the morning and says, "I don't want to go to work," or "I'm getting old." While you're thinking, you're forming pictures in your mind of the mostly negative thoughts and feelings that are coursing through your conscious mind. And if there's enough feeling behind those pictures, they'll be pushed to the subconscious mind and begin to dominate your daily life in a negative way. In time, they may manifest as disease, illness, addiction, and/or mental disorder.

That process can also work in a positive way, however, once you learn that you don't have to accept all the negative things that you've told yourself, or that others have said about you. You can begin to change that process by reprogramming your mind. In this chapter, I will discuss several techniques for this reprogramming, and give you a couple of brief exercises to help you get started.

### The Role of Faith in Healing

First, however, I need to say a few words about the role of faith in healing, and I'd like to begin with a series of scriptural quotations taken from the Gospels. To get something out of these quotations, you don't need to be a Christian or to believe that Jesus Christ was the only son of God. Whatever your religious belief system or mind-set, you can simply look at Jesus as a great healer and enlightened being on a par with the Buddha, Muhammad, Moses, Krishna, Lao-Tzu, or other great masters. I choose Jesus not only because he is my personal teacher and friend, but also because Jesus said several memorable things about the role of faith in healing. Once again, we're not talking about religious faith, or faith in the Bible or any religious dogma. When Jesus spoke of faith, he meant belief in the Divine within each of us that is synonymous with faith in one's connection with the Divine and confidence in the healing power of God. Here is some of what he said as recorded in the Gospels:

> *"Your faith has healed you."*
> *"As you believe, it shall be done unto you."*
> *"If you have faith, you could say to this mountain,*
> *'Depart' and it would obey you."*
> *"Pray believing you have [already] received and it will be*
> *done for you."*
> *"Your faith has made you whole."*
> *"Receive your sight; your faith has saved you."*

As St. Paul put it, every one of us is given a portion of faith. But that faith can be in either positive or negative results—we can believe that we will succeed or that we will fail. The mechanism is the same, but the outcome is different. As I've said, we have a choice as to what we put into the computer that is the mind. They say that the computer was designed to imitate the way the brain works. Are you still carrying hurts around with you? You have a choice to keep feeding those hurts into your computer or saying, "Today I'm going to get a healing for that. I'm going to let it go. I'm going to practice forgiveness. Not only am I going to forgive that person and that situation, but I'm also going to forgive myself for harboring these thoughts and feelings." By contemplating the opposite sense of our negative predispositions, we can actively reverse them, even if it means saying these decrees with feeling 20 times a day for weeks or months at a time.

You never have to be a victim again. You have a choice as to whether you love your body or hate it. I didn't know that for a long time, and I would say, for instance, if my back hurt, "Oh, that stinking back! That damn back, there it goes again, out of whack." And the pains would get worse. Then I heard an Episcopalian healer say that whenever you have a disease or pain in part of your body, don't attack it or say anything negative about it or to it. She said that instead, you could picture your hand as Jesus' hand, filled with light, lay it on the area that is in pain, and say, "I love you. I love you." It may sound strange, she said, but the greatest healing force in the world is love. Apply love as if you were applying an ointment to that diseased area, and then picture in your mind light surrounding that area— the healing light and love of God. It worked for me, and it will work for you—if you have faith.

Every emotion that surges or trickles through you causes a physical reaction somewhere in the body. A minor upset may take a couple of days to register as a headache or backache; a more vehement explosion of anger or hatred directed at someone could result in a terrible case of ulcers or colitis, because that emotion is pounding your body.

But just as negative emotions have a negative effect on the body, so too do positive emotions have a positive effect. You may have read in *Reader's Digest* or other popular magazines about the benefits of giving or receiving a certain number of hugs a day. We now know from scientific research that people who are involved in loving marriages and relationships live longer, on average, than people who live alone, because of the mental and physical support they give each other. Hugging and touching another person out of love helps the mind and emotions, as well as body chemistry. Joy and peace, which spring from love, help the nervous system function at an optimum level. The same has been found to be true of keeping pets. Even if you have no partner or loved ones living with you, you still have a need to give and share love, and we can do this with animals as well.

That's why whenever I lead a healing service or retreat, I always teach love first and foremost. When I pray with people, I think *love,* and I advise medical doctors that when they work with a patient, they do the same. When you're working with young children or talking to them before they go to sleep at night, think only *love.* Put your hand on them and allow your hand to be a vessel of love. When you hold hands with someone, think *love—God's* love, pure unconditional love. Not love *when,* or love *but,* or love *if*—just *love.*

### EXERCISE: AROUSING CHRIST CONSCIOUSNESS

The great psychologists Carl Jung and William James believed that we each possess not only a conscious and subconscious mind, but also a superconscious mind in which resides the infinite intelligence of God. This level of mind desires to work for and through the other two levels of the mind to produce good in one's life. What Jung and James refer to as *superconsciousness*, I prefer to call *Christ consciousness.* The reason I do is that Jesus seems to have known about and developed this miracle level of the mind, as reflected in his ministry, life, and teachings. I believe that all of us can develop this superconscious level of the mind by learning to dwell on attributes of the Christ consciousness. Psychologists tell us that we become what we focus our attention on. If we can learn to place our attention on our divinity—the Christ consciousness within us—we can begin to arouse that consciousness in the same way as the disciples of Jesus did. The early Christians released their superconscious power by meditating constantly on the name of Christ, specifically Christ Jesus.

The Hebrews released the superconscious power within them by meditating on the name of Jehovah, which they considered so sacred and powerful that they would not speak it aloud. They also used variations on the name of God, such as Jehovah Jireh, which means "God our Prosperity"; Jehovah Rapha, or "God our Health"; and Jehovah Shalom, or "God our Peace." The Hindus did much the same by chanting and meditating on the sacred sound *OM,* the creative element of God, which we might call the Holy Spirit.

The exercise that follows is a simple one to help you focus on a specific attribute of God so as to manifest awareness of that attribute in yourself—in this case, Christ consciousness as love consciousness. You can repeat the decree below a couple of times a day. To help you focus more intently, you may want to have someone else read it for you, or else speak it into a tape recorder and play it back while you relax with your eyes closed. Keep in mind, as I have said many times, that Jesus is for everyone. He is not about a particular religion, and it is certainly not necessary to be Christian to gain spiritual power from evoking his presence.

*"My consciousness is a consciousness of love. My consciousness has no desire for personal gain or glory. My consciousness is a channel through which God is flowing into the world. I am an instrument through which God's love blesses all people. My consciousness does not condemn others or myself. My consciousness does not seek revenge. My consciousness is a forgiving consciousness. Through my consciousness of love, which is the Christ consciousness, God enters my home, my career, my relationships, all that concerns me, as well as my nation and the whole universe. Because of this, I am blessed."*

### Reprogramming the Mind for Healing

When a marriage or relationship has gone sour, and all the counseling in the world can't save it because the spouses or partners are constantly at each other's throats, they sometimes continue to live together "for the kids' sake." But I know from working with those children that the parents are doing them more harm than if they went through the fire of separation or divorce. That couple can go to every seminar and workshop and read every book on self-esteem, but until they love themselves and share that love with others, there will be no change in the house. That lesson is contained in the story of the Canaanite woman told in the Gospel of Matthew (15:21-28). To understand the practical dimension of this story, you have to know that for historical and cultural reasons, the Jews despised the Canaanites, who worshiped sacred groves and statues of the Goddess, which the Israelites found reprehensible, and so they called the Canaanites dogs. Probably ever since this woman was a child, she had heard that term applied to her: "Get away from us, you dog!"

The Canaanite woman approaches Jesus and asks him to

heal her daughter, who is severely "possessed by a demon." In the version told in Matthew's gospel, he says that he was sent only to tend to the lost sheep of the House of Israel—but this statement does not appear in the Gospel of Mark, written before Matthew. When she persists, Jesus says, "It is not fair to take the children's bread and throw it to the dogs." I believe Jesus talked to her about dogs until she finally accepted the psychospiritual reality that she carried that hurt within her. In his wisdom, he knew it was foolish to heal the little child if the mother still cast off negative vibrations of bitterness when she got home. Finally, she says, "Yes, Lord, but even the dogs eat the crumbs that fall from their master's table." Then and only then does Jesus say, "O woman, great is your faith! Be it done for you as you desire." And her daughter is healed. As in so many other instances in the Gospels, faith leads to healing.

Parents often bring their children to me for healing because they've already been to places such as the Mayo Clinic and been told that the child's illness has "no physical cause." Usually I send the child out of the room and talk to the parents, asking them to tell me what their home life is like—and most of the time it's terrible. More than likely, the psychological and emotional disruption at home is creating symptoms for which no genetic or physical cause exists. And so Jesus had to heal the negative sting in the memory of the Canaanite woman, her bitter feelings and resentment, before he could do anything for the child.

While all of our thoughts go into the subconscious, not all of them have an effect on us. If not all of our thinking triggers a response in the body, what makes the difference? Those that affect us most enter our subconscious through the powerful emotion of fear. If you had a traumatic, fearful experience at age three or four, you have never forgotten it.

When I was five years old, I was taken to the hospital to have a mastoid operation on my throat. To this day, I can vividly see that nurse standing over me, and my hand reaching up. I was so scared that I literally ripped the top buttons off her uniform, because I didn't know what was going to happen. In those days, they didn't tell kids anything before an operation, because they thought that was best. But the result was a tremendously frightful experience that registered in my subconscious and remains there to this day. I have, however, been able to heal the memory of that fear—not by removing the memory, but by exorcising the emotional sting connected to that memory, as I described to you earlier.

We can see an example of this in the story of the demoniac whom Christ heals in the Gospel of Mark (5:17). In those days, they referred to epilepsy, schizophrenia, and other diseases they did not understand as being possessed by a demon. (The Greeks used the word *daemonai* to denote a spiritual energy that controls one. For a more comprehensive discussion of this term, see *Prayer and the Five Stages of Healing*, chapter 6). Jesus is talking with his disciples when all of a sudden a naked man runs through the cemetery, picking up pieces of rock and scratching his neck and face. The people couldn't do anything with him, but Jesus noticed the man and undoubtedly looked at him with love. When that man saw Jesus looking at him, he saw love and the power to heal. Jesus just reached out and touched him, perhaps the first time in many years that anyone had touched him other than in a vain attempt to restrain him. At that moment, I believe, the man received God's love and was healed.

The young boy whose father brings him to Jesus in the ninth chapter of Mark has been rolling around in the bonfires set in the countryside. Jesus let the boy be and began to talk to the father. How long has he been this way? When did this begin to happen? Jesus wanted to first calm the father and show his concern for the young boy, who was probably an epileptic. When the boy stood up, Jesus touched him and loved him, because the laying on of hands is nothing if not an act of love, and in doing so, he healed him. Reaching out and drawing people into the love of God *has to* help heal them, especially if they haven't been touched in years.

To get a response out of the brain's computer, there must be something special about the information entering the subconscious. You need three special elements to get a reaction in the body: what you imagine (what you see in your mind); what you believe; and your feelings. When you begin to program your mind with good thoughts, those positive thoughts get rid of the negative. You never give up smoking by concentrating on giving up smoking. You never lose weight and leave it off by concentrating on weight. Instead, you need to focus on what your life will be like without cigarettes, on what you will do with the money you save, and on how healthy you will feel (and be). You have to focus on being your ideal weight, on the wonderful, nourishing foods you'll eat. When you concentrate on the good, it doesn't make any difference why you gained the weight or why you smoked. The good replaces the harmful thing that's going on in your life.

One of the reasons I use audiocassette tapes and recommend them to others is that I've seen how they work in my life—not just my own tapes, but all of the tapes that people create to help us develop positive vibrations within. When you begin to see yourself as God sees you, when you reprogram your mind with the good thoughts He has for us, then you will see progress. The plans that He has for us are plans for good, not for evil. So just let negativity go. You may not know the cause of something, but you know that something is wrong in your life. You can see the wrong and you will sit down and meditate, and nothing seems to come to you as to what has caused this problem. Well, just let that experience of the wrong go. It doesn't make any difference what caused it because too much introspection isn't good for you either. You always have to keep a balance.

About 17 years ago, I bought a set of tapes by the well-known personal coach Denis Waitley, called *The Psychology of Winning*, and each title was a reminder of what I didn't have within myself: "Positive Self-Expectancy," "Positive Self-Image," "Positive Self-Control," Positive Self-Esteem," "Positive Self-Awareness," "Positive Self-Motivation," "Positive Self-Direction," "Positive Self-Discipline," and "Positive Self-Projection." Not long before listening to those tapes, I had left a parish I didn't like, fully expecting that I'd probably repeat the process—and, of course, I did. I thought I would probably get another pastor who didn't understand me, and I got one. What you believe and expect really does happen. I knew I was no good and so I wasn't, and I wasn't any good to my people either. I had no control. When I got up in that pulpit to talk and I saw someone look at his watch, he became my target. I would aim my howitzer right at him. Every time I got up in the morning, my only motivation was, "Here we go again."

Around the same time I was using the Waitley tapes, I was also beginning to listen to the world-famous television minister Robert Schuller, and between the two of them, something down deep inside of me began to say, "This is possible. This is really possible. I don't have to be miserable. I can change!"

It wasn't easy at first, because every part of my previous training fought against it. But then one day as I was listening to the tapes, I remembered what I'd studied at a Benedictine seminary in Missouri. My moral theology teacher had been taught by a wonderful theologian based in Rome named Bernard Häring, who was quite radical for his time. We used a four-volume set of his teachings in class, and the first year we studied the love of God—how to *receive* love from God and how to give love *back* to God. In the second year, we studied how to love yourself. The third year was all about loving one another after we've received God's love and learned to love ourselves. And during the fourth year, we studied a summary of the first three. As I was listening to those tapes and recalling my courses in moral theology, I thought, *My God, this is theologically sound and correct.*

I'm not certain why I needed the confirmation of a Catholic theologian that it was all right to make use of secular self-improvement technology. To begin with, of course, Häring himself was an extraordinary individual. Considered by many to be the most significant figure in Catholic moral theology in the second half of the 20th century, he was a pioneer in the modern church. While he was still a young priest in Hitler's Germany, Häring was drafted into World War II as an army medic. His spiritual commitment led him to defy orders forbidding him to say Mass, and to risk his life to minister to refugees, Jewish concentration camp inmates, and enemy soldiers.

Häring's most famous work, *Free and Faithful in Christ*, is a pioneering work of moral theology that proposed a code of moral conduct that is life-centered rather than sin-centered. My being exposed to his revolutionary thinking in the relatively conservative environment of a Roman Catholic seminary was in itself a gift of grace. But whatever the reason, my emotional health began to improve markedly as I opened myself to the synergistic possibilities suggested by Häring, Waitley, and Schuller. On reflection, I was able to assemble the underlying principles that I learned while experiencing the work of these three men.

### Principles of Healing

1. *"As one thinks in his heart, so is he"* (Proverbs 23:7). When the Hebrew Bible talks about "heart," it is referring to the subconscious or inner being. I can't reiterate this principle enough, and it could be expressed in modern terms, "As one feels in his inner being, so is he." As Denis Waitley put it,

we don't necessarily get what we *want* in life, but we do get what we *expect*. If you expect to fail, you probably will—no matter how hard you try to succeed.

**2.** Scientific and psychological research has determined that **the conscious mind is the guardian of the subconscious,** the gateway to the inner computer. Since it can be shown that the subconscious reacts to ideas flowing into it, the conscious mind becomes the control knob of the subconscious computer. Whatever the conscious mind believes, the subconscious accepts as fact. Indeed, the function of the subconscious is to accept material as it comes from the conscious and store it for future reference. The subconscious makes no judgments as to whether material it is given is good or bad, true or false.

**3. What the subconscious accepts as fact, it seeks to express in the body of its owner**. The subconscious reacts impersonally to information it receives from the conscious mind. It will carry out a damaging or false idea as readily as a beneficial or true one. If a person believes that she is the victim of a certain illness, the subconscious will do its best to see that the symptoms of that illness are manifested in her body. On the other hand, if that same person receives positive input somewhere along the line, that can influence the rest of her life in a constructive way.

My father worked as a highway engineer and sometimes drove a road grader, an enormous machine used to level an entire roadway. Every so often, he would drive it home for lunch and let me get behind the wheel. That gave me such an astounding feeling of power and control that many years later, getting up in front of an audience of 10,000 and leading a healing service did not seem frightening. Did my father know he was doing this, or was he just proud of his work? It doesn't matter, although I believe that on a semiconscious or subconscious level, he wanted to transmit that feeling of power and mastery to his son.

**4. The more deeply the subconscious is impressed with a fact or belief, the faster it will try to carry it out.** Ideas from the conscious mind affect the subconscious according to the amount of emotion behind them. Emotion is like the gunpowder in a bullet or a projectile: The more there is, the faster and more powerfully it will fly.

**5. The subconscious always acts in accordance with the current beliefs of the conscious mind.** For example, if we're sick and trying to heal, but we believe that God is out to get us or that we somehow deserve to be punished, the chances are that we will not be healed. Whatever we believe to be the attributes of the Divine determines how we will act in life. If we see God as an authoritarian Father who withholds His love, we may have trouble believing that He will answer our prayers. Therefore, they most likely won't be answered to our liking. If we've always thought of God as a powerful masculine figure, then we may have trouble comprehending God as a tender, compassionate, nurturing Being. All conceptions of God do not have to be masculine. In Hebrew, one of the names of God is El Shaddai, which means "The Full-Breasted One."

**6. The subconscious responds to one's imagination, not to one's will.** Most people have a problem giving up negative or destructive behavior—not because they don't want to, but because they can't let go of past imprinting that lives in their imagination. Somebody convinced them that they're losers, that they'll never amount to a hill of beans, that they're not good with numbers, that they can't sing a note, that they read too much or think too much. It doesn't do any good to tell people who have a problem with drinking not to drink;

the subconscious hears only "drink," and tells the mind it needs one.

Warren Spahn was pitching a no-hitter in the World Series when the coach walked out to the mound and told him that the next hitter kills the ball low and inside. Whatever you do, the coach said, don't give him a low inside pitch. Spahn couldn't help doing just that, and the guy hit a home run and won the game for the other team.

As great as the Ten Commandments are, they still tend to make you focus too much on negativity. Jesus chose to focus on the positive attribute of love. If you truly love, you won't commit adultery; if you love, you won't steal or kill or bear false witness. That's why the greatest Commandment is "Love the Lord your God, and love your neighbor as you love yourself." Everything else follows from that. If you just focus on not killing and not stealing, you may lead a virtuous life, but you may never contribute anything of value to the community.

A person can will to be healed, but such efforts are usually futile. You can will all you like, but nothing will happen, because our mental computer responds mainly to sensory images and emotion-filled words. How, then, should you go about being healed? To take a specific example, let's say that you have liver cancer. You don't picture the liver in your mind the way it looks now, or the fact that your skin is turning jaundiced, or focus on the pain. You picture the liver as whole and healthy. You picture all the things you would do if you were healed. You might picture that whole area of your body filled with light. But it does no good to picture a healthy liver and then keep thinking, *I probably won't get healed. I'll probably stay sick.* You're negating the prayer. So watch what you say, watch what you think, and watch what you picture.

One thing you can do is to see the problem and bring Jesus into it. If you don't feel comfortable with Jesus for any reason, then choose a sacred figure with whom you feel a close connection. It could be the Buddha or another figure from Buddhist culture, such as Padma Sambhava or the Dalai Lama. It could be any image of the Goddess, such as Mary, the Mother of Jesus; the Indian Mother Goddess Uma; the Tibetan goddess Tara; or Quanyin, the Chinese *boddhisattva* of compassion. Because Jesus is my master, I am most comfortable visualizing him, so I would advise you to let Jesus walk into the situation and then just talk to him. You'll begin to get ideas, thoughts, and hunches as if Jesus were talking to you personally, in the flesh. Through his Spirit, he actually *is* speaking to you and giving you guidance and wisdom.

If you have an emotional or behavioral problem, don't fight it. Turn it into a challenge and an opportunity; say that you can overcome this and then bring Jesus into it. Whenever you picture Jesus or any other sacred being in a situation, it has a calming effect on your mind and body. If you go to the doctor, for example, and he tells you that you have a tumor or cancer, the natural reaction is to panic. If your loved one comes home screaming and panicking, don't tell her to stop; let her get it out of her system first. You just listen. And then put your arms around her and bring Jesus or your sacred being into the situation. That will have a calming effect.

When I get tense and I can feel those muscles in the shoulder saying, "Let's get this guy," then I have to stop and bring Jesus into it. Usually I picture a location that has a calming effect on me, such as the ocean, or a lake in springtime. Then I'll see myself sitting there as Jesus comes walking along the beach and sits down to talk with me. That little exercise gives me the enthusiasm to get up and go on with my work. Clearly, if you need medical help, if you're so sick that you can't even do a mental exercise, then you should go to the doctor. Use everything God has made available for you. But never stop using your mind and imagination to initiate or complement healing.

The will is not a part of the material flowing into the

subconscious, but is a part of the decision-making apparatus. When the will and the imagination are in conflict, the imagination always wins. What you picture, wins. For example, take the line from Jeremiah, in which God says, "I know the plans I have for you are plans for good, not of evil. They are plans to bring you a future and a hope." As you're reading that, close your eyes and picture everything that has gone wrong in your life for the last five years. Will that Scripture verse sink down in your subconscious and affect your life for the better? You can sit there willing it to do so until you're blue in the face, but as long as you keep picturing all the so-called evil that has happened in your life recently, nothing beneficial will happen.

That's why when you pray with others who are sick, don't concentrate on their illness. Let them say "I have cancer," and then drop it. Just pray for their overall well-being, and never bring up the illness again. You get their mind and their picture apparatus working as best you can. The imagination was created by God as the playground of the Holy Spirit. Our words plus our imagination—the way we picture things—plus the Holy Spirit, brings good into our life.

When you read the Scriptures, stop and picture it happening to you in your mind, which is a form of meditation. This is the same process that Ignatius of Loyola, in his work *Spiritual Exercises*, called "mental representation of place." Ignatius recommends progressively focusing on the subject of meditation like the zoom lens of a camera; at other times he advises pulling back to focus on the larger picture.[1] The key here is to feel free to visualize what's happening in the Scriptures you read in whatever way helps you feel connected to the subject of your visualization. If you want healing, take a passage that might refer to a disease you're suffering from. If you have a problem with your legs, find a passage in the Scriptures where Jesus heals a paralyzed person (even if your ailment is not paralysis, it could be anything related—from arthritic joints to psoriasis). Then picture yourself in that man's position, and let Jesus touch you. *But use your imagination.*

When the will and the imagination are in conflict, the imagination always wins.

**7. Hope, faith, and love working together are necessary for maximum benefit to the human being in regard to exhilarating relationships, rewarding careers, healthy living, and abundance.**

### Exercise: Healing Past Hurts

Since many of the exercises in this book involve using your imagination to picture something in your mind, I'd like to put you at ease about this simple technique. Although it is commonly called "visualization," you don't need to see a crystal-clear image in your mind's eye. Whether trying to imagine Jesus, some other sacred being, or just a golden light, most people see at best a hazy holographic image that may barely resemble anything very clearly. The important thing is the intention to call up the sacred image or the healing light—not the specific form of it.

Keeping this in mind, close your eyes, relax, take a few deep breaths, or use any of the relaxation techniques you're comfortable with. You may want to have someone read this to you, or you may record it first and then play it back as you do the exercise.

Envision yourself seated near a lake on a lovely clear day, engulfed in a glorious, warm white light that glows as radiantly as thousands of diamonds. Sense that this light is God's Holy Spirit, and bathe in it for a few minutes. Then with your inner eye of faith and trust, see Jesus standing before you smiling. See yourself as he embraces you and calls you by name: "I love you, _____ . I want to help you. I want to restore you and heal you. I want you to experience a full and abundant life."

Simply accept this from Jesus as true, with an attitude of gratitude. State your gratitude either verbally or silently, such as "Thank you, Jesus, for revealing this to me."

At this point, Jesus reminds you of some hurts that are preventing you from being fully alive. These hurts were inflicted on you by people in your past, and you can sense these people now standing next to you in the light—yes, they're in the light because God loves them, also. See Jesus embracing these people. Visualize them crying as Jesus embraces and forgives them.

Jesus is smiling as he looks at you and asks you to do the same, as difficult as this may be for you. Remembering that this is for your healing, embrace the person(s) you believe hurt you. Tell them "I, _____ [your name], forgive you. Will you _____, [their name], please forgive me, especially for my harboring judgmental, nonloving thoughts toward you?"

Envision yourself embracing each other with love. Sense a joy beginning to well up within you, no matter how slight it may seem. Feel the peace that is beginning to emanate from your inner being. As that sense of peace begins to engulf you like a tide of warm ocean water, take three deep breaths and slowly open your eyes.

You can begin to practice this visualization in your daily prayer time and experience what it means to put on the mind of Christ, a mind of love and peace, joy and forgiveness, which sees the world as good and loving in all its aspects.

---

[1] For more details on Loyola's technique, consult the Introduction to my book *I Want to See Jesus in a New Light.*

# Chapter Five

❧ ❧

# Holiness and Wholeness

In the Gospel of Matthew (5:48), Jesus says, "Be perfect therefore as your heavenly Father is perfect." That sounds fairly daunting, since none of us is or can ever be perfect. What is Jesus really asking for? A more accurate translation of the continuous Greek form is, "Go on being perfected as your heavenly Father is perfect." But the Greek word generally translated as *perfect* actually means "completed" or "whole." So an even more faithful rendering would be, "Go on being made whole, as your heavenly Father is whole." Another way of saying that is, "Be compassionate and all-inclusive, just as God is compassionate and includes everyone in His love."

In the previous chapter, I discussed the connection between the body and the mind—both the conscious and subconscious mind—in the healing process. Now we need to understand these connections as parts of a whole. To be whole means to dwell in the spiritual realm—that is, to live, move, and have our being in the energy of the Divine Spirit. It means to be harmonized in the physical body; in the mind—which has control of the will and the emotions—and in the Spirit, which is what Jesus is talking about when he tells us to be compassionate and all-inclusive.

## Using the Laws of Healing for Yourself

Before you go out and try to bring healing to others, bring it to yourself. The sacred Scriptures of all the great spiritual traditions show us the best way to heal ourselves, to bring wholeness and abundant living. But we must always remember that we are not just spirit, we are not just body, and we are not just soul. We are all of that in one. Still, because we are human, we have to approach each of these areas separately, at least at first.

Beginning with the mind, as we have just seen, the surest way to health is through a positive outlook. I believe the first "positive thinking" book ever written was Paul's Letter to the Philippians, especially the passage in chapter 4:4-9. Paul is telling the congregation to refocus their minds on the positive: "Rejoice in the Lord always; I will say it again, Rejoice. Let your gentleness, your kindness be evident to all. The Lord is near. Do not be anxious about anything but in everything by prayer and petition with thanksgiving, let your requests be known to God. And the peace of God, which transcends all understanding, will guard your hearts and your minds. Finally, whatever is true, whatever is noble, whatever is right, whatever is pure, whatever is lovely, whatever is admirable, if anything is excellent, then think about these things."

"Whatever is pure" means "whatever is sincere." Our English word *sincere* is believed by some etymologists to be derived from the Latin words *sine cera,* meaning "without wax." In the early culture of Greece and Rome, to save money they sometimes used wax as a filler in building materials, and the oldest meaning of *sincere* is "unmixed" or "unadulterated." So to be sincere means to be without any kind of phony filler.

In the Gospel of Mark (11:24), Jesus says to his disciples, "Whatever you ask in prayer, believe that you receive it, and you will." He's talking about seeing or sensing what you want to accomplish or be so that it becomes reality. When I begin this process, I relax by putting my attention on a picture I call the Laughing Jesus, a line drawing of Jesus having an uproariously good laugh—not an image normally purveyed by the Christian church. I may also focus on the Catholic image of the Sacred Heart of Jesus, on fire with love for humanity; or simply on the heart of Jesus, because it represents God's unconditional love for us. After a while, you'll get so adept that you won't need to begin this way. You'll just be able to relax as you begin consciously breathing in the way I explained earlier. Once you accept God's unconditional love for you, you can begin to love yourself. When you begin to love yourself, you can share that love with others.

It's difficult to feel positive in your mind, however, if your body is tense or out of synch. If you have difficulty relaxing, you'll have to talk to your body. Start from the top of your head, remembering what Jesus said when there was a tremendous storm around him in the sea: "Peace, be still." If any of the parts of your body are uncomfortable, tense, or full of anxiety, begin to speak to that part of your body: "Peace, be still. Peace, be still." So if you feel a tension in your shoulders, you might say to yourself, "Peace, be still, shoulders." Call them by their name. If you have a headache, then say, "Head, peace, be still, relax." If your eyes are fluttering all over the place because you can't control your muscles, tell them to be still. You can do the same thing with pain. If you have a pain resulting from a disease, say, "Peace, be still, relax."

Begin this technique very simply, perhaps focusing on a picture or statue of Jesus or Mary or some other sacred image, or a word of Jesus from the Scriptures, which can have a tremendous calming and soothing quality. The *Song of Solomon* from the Old Testament, says: "Your name, O Lord, is like perfumed oil poured out." So when you want to relax, think of the name of Jesus (or Mary, Buddha, Tara, Uma, and so on).

As you're relaxing, you're thinking of Jesus, but you're also seeing a picture of him in your mind. You're seeing Jesus come out of that picture and maybe put his arms around you and kiss you on the cheek. At first it may be difficult to visualize all that—if you grew up in a Christian church, you may have mixed feelings about Jesus. However, after a while, it will become easier. In the Hindu tradition, the act of repeating or meditating on the names of God is known as *namas marana*. The living Indian saint Sai Baba encourages people to focus on an image of any God-realized being while saying the names of God.

At the same time, you must also practice affirmative prayer, saying, for instance, "Yes, the Spirit is here. The Spirit is here right now. The Spirit is my healing power. The Spirit is working miracles in my life right now." You can also use your own name, as I do when I pray this way: "Ron, the Spirit's power is filling you full. Ron, the Spirit's power is taking away that pain."

The more you visualize, the more you will affirm; the more you affirm, the more you will meditate; the more you meditate, the more you will relax. When you're finished, begin to thank God. Never end your prayers without thanksgiving, because that's a release of positive faith that what you're doing is working.

Practice this art every morning when you get up and every night when you go to bed, and you will see your whole life change at such a rapid pace that it will surprise you. But don't wait too long at night to meditate; catch yourself as you're starting to get tired and say, "I'd better turn this TV program off and go meditate, because I need to make sure my mind is calm and tranquil before I go to sleep."

Keeping in mind that the keys to success in this art are Desire, Determination, and Discipline, let me take you through a brief meditation so you can see how this works. You can either read the following exercise as you go along, stopping every so often to close your eyes and get into the spirit of it, or you can prerecord it on a cassette and then relax and do the exercise as you play back the tape.

## A Brief Meditation and Relaxation Exercise

In this meditation, once again I use the image of Jesus because it's the one I'm most familiar and comfortable with. But you may substitute the image of any manifestation of Divinity or any God-realized teacher to whom you feel a special connection.

> *The body is relaxing. The mind is relaxing. All negative thoughts are being released. I am at peace. I am one with God. I sense His peace. I sense His love, His joy. I see above my head a glorious, brilliant ball of light. It is descending into my head, lighting up my forehead . . . my eyes . . . nose . . . mouth . . . throat . . . neck . . . shoulders . . . arms . . . hands . . . stomach . . . back . . . waist. It's lighting up every part of my body . . . genitals . . . legs . . . knees . . . ankles . . . feet. The light is God's relaxing light. I am one with that light, and I'm at peace. In that light emanating from my body, I see golden rays going outward. The golden rays are surrounding an image in front of me. It's Jesus, and I'm looking at him now. His beautiful eyes are shining, his mouth is upturned in a glorious smile, and I hear him say to me, "I love you. I love you."*
>
> *He is holding out his arms to me, and now I run into those arms. As he embraces me, I feel one with Jesus. All the strength of Jesus, all the power of Jesus, all the peace of Jesus is filling every part of my body, mind, and spirit. It's activating the Holy*

*Spirit within me. "The word of the Lord went forth and healed them," say the Scriptures. He heals all of my infirmities and takes away all of my iniquities and sin.*

*Think about the man who wanted healing and went up to Jesus and said, "If you want to, you could heal me." Jesus said, "I want to; be healed." Talk to Jesus. Say something like, "I accept the healing power that you give me, Jesus, because you want to do this. You love me and you want to do this. Thank you."*

∽◊∾

With a positive mind and a relaxed body, you are ready to approach your spirit. If you want a job done, affirm Divine Spirit. Manifest the perfect ideas to produce this work quickly and efficiently. It's good to repeat your affirmations three times—one for the body, one for the mind, and one for the spirit. And as you affirm, picture or sense the Divine Spirit working for you and with you. If you will invest ten minutes a day, picturing the Divine Spirit at work in your business, in your family affairs, or even in personalities who might rub you the wrong way, the results will amaze you. If you're having difficulty with a particular person, for example, see that person embraced by a golden light, and sense the person expressing happiness. This will activate the love of God and the peace of God within you and the person. To become a better individual yourself, affirm, using your own name:

"I, _____ , behold the Christ Spirit in you. I behold the Christ Light at work in your life, producing perfect results now. My life cannot be limited. The Christ Energy in me is my freeing, healing, loving, prospering power."

Imagine, visualize, affirm. Every part of that trinity is essential to success. It's not enough to affirm words; you must have powerful emotions behind them. They have to be something you can picture in your mind. "The Christ Spirit in me is my forgiving power. The Christ Spirit in me frees me from all attachments that will hinder my growth toward wholeness. The Christ Spirit in me is my healing power. This Divine energy in me now raises me up to perfect health. The Christ Spirit is producing perfect results in every phase of my life now, and all is well. I relax. I let go."

Imagine, visualize, affirm. If you have trouble visualizing abstract concepts such as "forgiving power" or "healing power," don't let it bother you. When in doubt, I always imagine Jesus or some Divine being, angel, or saint giving me a big hug. That Divine gesture embraces forgiveness, healing, abundance, and just about every other positive thought, feeling, or attribute.

### Prayer As Positive Affirmation

As you utilize the principles I've been explaining, you'll begin to experience them. Sometimes when you pray with one or more people, the best thing to do is take them by the hand and visualize that the hand you're holding is the hand of Jesus or some Divine being, angel, or saint; and that power and peace and healing are coming from that hand through your body, your mind, and activating your spirit.

When you make affirmations of peace, the first thing that happens when you begin to think about a Divine Being is that a great calm descends upon you. You begin to feel better about everything in your life. Here is where tapes such as those of Denis Waitley have come in handy for me in the past, because as your subconscious grows calm, it will accept whatever is going into it, as long as those words are backed by powerful, emotion-packed affirmations and visualizations.

You have to take responsibility for your life. You have to

decide what you want out of life and then go after it. That's what I do. That's why goal setting is important. You have to have a vision of what you want to accomplish in life. If you have no vision, then don't be surprised when you miss life because you've set nothing to aim at. As it says in the Book of Proverbs (29:18): "Where there is no vision, the people perish." A human being is built by God so wondrously that each of us is like a homing device. If all we think about is sickness and ill health, we're going to head in that direction. If we think resentment, if we think fear, if we have anxiety attacks, we're heading for destruction.

Prayer isn't so much *doing* as *being* with someone—namely, with God. It's experiencing love and peace. But if you've been restless all of your life or have been filled with resentment and bitterness, you'll miss peace of mind even when it's dropped in your lap.

When talking about the role of prayer in healing, we have to begin by remembering that the most powerful prayer is positive decree based on God's word. One of my favorite affirmations comes right out of Scripture, from the Letter of Paul to Philippians. "I can do all things through Christ's Spirit, which strengthens me." That's a powerful affirmation, but if you don't see yourself accomplishing good things in your mind, you can say that until you're blue in the face and nothing is going to change. Things will only get worse, because you'll get more frustrated. Even as you're saying, "I can do all things through Christ's Spirit, which strengthens me," your subconscious says, "No I can't!" The reason is that in your subconscious are all of the recordings of rejection, and all the years that you heard, "You're no good." You've accepted that, and you still accept it. I don't care what you say on the outside; you carry that into the world like a flashing neon light. The moment you walk into a crowd, your light is either flashing "I am good" or "I am no good."

Jesus prayed the powerful prayer of positive decree when

he raised Lazarus from the dead in the Gospel of John (11:40-41). When Jesus arrived on the scene and asked to have the tomb opened, Lazarus had already been dead four days. His sisters Mary and Martha said he would already be smelling of decay, but Jesus said, "Did I not tell you that if you believed, you would see the glory of God?" Then they took away the stone from the grave of Lazarus, and Jesus looked up and said, "Father, I thank you that you have heard me."

Perhaps Jesus visualized what was about to take place and heard the Father say to him, "It is done." At the top of his voice, Jesus said, "Lazarus, come out!" And when Lazarus appeared, Jesus taught a very important message in just one statement: "Unbind him and let him go free." I am not a Biblical scholar, but I have always found it curious that the story of Lazarus appears only in the Gospel of John, written some 70 or 80 years after the fact. Actually raising someone from the dead is the kind of miracle that would have been trumpeted in all the Gospels, more so than simply healing a paralytic or casting out demons. For that reason, I've always taken this story symbolically. The graveclothes around Lazarus are symbols of negative emotions that rot our being from the inside out, and by his words and actions, Jesus—or the author of that Gospel—is telling us to unbind ourselves of our negative trappings and go free.

We find another example of Jesus' affirmative prayer in the Gospel of Mark (8:6ff), a story better known as the multiplication of the loaves and fishes. After Jesus told the crowd that had been listening to him preach all day to sit down on the ground, he took the seven loaves that his disciples had gathered and immediately gave thanks. He didn't say, "Lord, Father, these guys are hungry. Could you multiply these loaves?" He didn't petition at all. He broke the loaves and gave them to his disciples to set before the people. They had a few small fish as well. But Jesus didn't say, "Father, would you multiply the fish?" He simply gave thanks again and told the disciples to distribute them.

Finally, we have what is called commonly the Lord's Prayer, or the Our Father, which is a prayer not of petition but of sheer affirmation. I have written extensively on the Our Father in my other books, primarily in *The Healing Path of Prayer* (for a detailed explanation, see chapter 4 of that book). Some notable Aramaic scholars have shown that the Lord's Prayer changes substantially when one examines how it was most likely said in the original Aramaic that Jesus spoke. The major difference is that what has become a petitionary prayer ("Give us this day our daily bread") was originally a prayer of affirmation ("You do give us our daily sustenance"). Here I have used that basic Aramaic-derived text as a template from which to expand and improvise more comprehensive versions of the prayer, attempting to plumb its meaning and implications on several levels. For comparison, I have included the relevant lines of the standard translation of the Lord's Prayer in parentheses.

*Our Father-Mother, whose Divine love, presence, energy, or vibration fills the whole universe.* (Our Father who art in heaven.).

*May we take this frequency, this vibration, this energy into our being as into a temple, for it to reside at all times.* (Hallowed be thy name.)

*Your authority, your power, your presence, your spirit, your essence come forth in me now.* (Thy Kingdom come, thy will be done.)

*And let it be in the world of matter as it is in the world of spirit.* (On earth as it is in heaven.)

*You do give us this day that which we need to feed our emotions, our bodies, our relationships, every aspect of our life. That is the "bread" you give us, O Father, O Divine Mother.* (Give us this day our daily bread.)

*You do forgive us in the very same way that we*

*forgive others. The energy that goes out in our forgiveness of others comes back to us tenfold, 60-fold, 100-fold.* (Forgive us our trespasses as we forgive those who trespass against us.)

*And being a loving Spirit, a loving Essence, a loving Father, a loving Mother, you do not let us become attached to superficial things, but you separate us from anything that might hold us back.* (Lead us not into temptation, but deliver us from evil.)

*Amen.*

The word translated as "evil" in the final passage does not mean that at all, but rather means "error." The phrase "You deliver us from error" refers to the erroneous ways in which we speak to and interact with others. After I started to pray this way from my own heart using the "Our Father" as an outline, everything else began to change.

When I was studying theology at that Benedictine monastery in the small Missouri town of Conception Junction, one of my professors was a translator of the Dead Sea Scrolls. Father Ignatius Hunt, O.S.B., was the most humble man I've ever met, despite his two Ph.D.'s in Sanskrit and Aramaic and in Sacred Scripture. Right across the street from the monastery was the parish grammar school, where he would walk into a classroom with young kids, sit on the floor, and talk to them about God in a language they could understand. Then Father Hunt would cross the street, walk into a class of theologians, and speak to us on our level. He also taught in the college religion department. He was the only priest I ever knew who, when he celebrated any sacred ritual, smiled all the way through it. You just knew he "knew" something. Better yet, you knew he knew *someone*.

This man was my spiritual director for four years, and he always said that whenever you study Scriptures, you must keep in mind the *Sitz im Leben*. That's a German term used in theological circles to denote "the situation in life at the time the text was written." You cannot translate it with today's mind! You must translate it in terms of what was occurring when it was written.

That means that you can't understand the Our Father until you get some basic understanding of what the language meant to the people. Aramaic is a language of sacred sound. Jesus spoke Aramaic because the common people spoke Aramaic, but the priests in the Temple spoke Hebrew. In much the same way, in later times, the Roman Catholic clergy and theologians communicated in Latin, or Hindu brahmans in Sanskrit, even though the common people no longer understood those ancient tongues. So when Jesus spoke to the people, there would be certain inflections in the same word that would change its whole meaning.

Take the word *abwoon*, translated "Father," or "Our Father." Unlike English words, *abwoon* is broken into four frequencies or vibrations. Jesus said, "When you pray, pray, AH-BW-OO-OON." And those sounds would immediately tell the person, "AH, the sound of God. The sound of the omnipotent Being, the all-pure Being." The sound BW conveys energy emanation; OO represents blessings coming forth from God on the wings of the Spirit, the wings of breath, to interpenetrate—OON—matter, and create something new. So it isn't just "Our Father." It's AH-BW-OO-OON, and that's how the people understood it. But we don't get it today because we've lost the history and the understanding of what the words meant to the people when Jesus spoke them.

Here is yet another paraphrasing of what Jesus was saying in the Lord's Prayer in my own words. You can, of course, substitute either of these versions for the traditional prayer.

*Our Daddy, who is unlimited, sanctified be your name; may it be held in high esteem within me. Your kingdom of love and peace and joy, power and abundance, come into me. Your will be done. You save the lost and heal the sick. That is your will. O Lord, I thank you, for I sense that you have saved me from myself; you have healed me, you have made me whole. For once I was lost, but now I am found. You give us this day everything we need to sustain and maintain our lives, everything we need in mind, body, and spirit. You release us from our faults and errors, for that's your desire. You have wired us uniquely by allowing us to release ourselves from negative energies and emotions by releasing others. So you do forgive us as we forgive, as we let go, as we bless. That is what you mean when you tell us that we are to bless others—circumstances, situations, and people that we perceive have hurt us. But, Father/Mother, no one can hurt me unless I give them the power in my mind and accept that hurt from them. No one can hurt me because you have taught me to live in your Spirit, and yours is an all-powerful Spirit. You do not lead us into temptation, for you would be a wicked God to lead us purposely into a situation just so you could kick us and beat us while we're down. That is not the God of love displayed in the Scriptures. You deliver us from error so that we can shine forth the light of your love and peace and joy, and the world will see it. For thine is the kingdom and the power and the glory, now and forever.*[1]

In my opinion, that is the way the Our Father was intended to be prayed—with power and with confidence. In the Gospel of John, chapter 15, Jesus again tells us how to approach the Father as he himself would: "As the Father has loved me, so have I loved you. Now remain in my love. If you will obey my commands, you will remain in my love just as I have obeyed my Father's commands and remain in His love. I have told you this so that my joy may be in you, and your joy may be complete."

When Jesus says in John 16:24, "I tell you the truth; my Father will give you whatever you ask in my name," he means that this will occur whenever you go to the Father/Mother with the same understanding he has. You cannot go with anger, resentment, bitterness, or anxiety in your heart. You must go with peace, in love, and with an enthusiasm that says it's going to work! In other words, we must learn to go to the Divine Father/Mother as if Jesus himself—in us—was doing it. He didn't go with petitions, but with thanksgiving, confidence, and trust.

### The Choice Is Yours

The underlying theme of this book is learning to take responsibility for your life, which implies opening up to the Spirit of God so that the Spirit can guide and guard you. You can't take responsibility for your life if you blame your family or your religious organization whenever things go wrong. Years ago, I was very heavily involved in the blame game. If anything went wrong in my life, I would find something or someone to pin it on. You may think that the moment you do that, you'll feel better, but you don't. So you find somebody else to blame for that feeling, too. You don't feel better, so you look for more people in still other situations to blame, and the feelings become progressively worse. You have a choice to continue down that road or to give up the blame game and live. I believe that whenever something potentially upsetting happens to us in life, we can either see it as a judgment of God or fate, or as an opportunity to grow. As the Lord says in Deuteronomy, "I lay before you life and death, blessings and curses. Choose life."

## EXERCISE: CHOOSE LIFE

Realizing that the choice is always yours, make the commitment now to be more aware of what you think and say on a minute-by-minute basis, and to try in each situation, in each moment, to choose the positive rather than the negative. To help you with this process, try the following multipart exercise. It's best to do the entire exercise in the morning so that you can carry the awareness it generates through the day with you. In this exercise—and you can create others like it—begin with the selected readings from Scripture, then take a moment to reflect on the deeper meaning of those words. Next, say a prayer drawn from your reflection. Then create a positive affirmation based on the reflection and prayer. Finally, devise some way in which you can put the sentiments sketched out in the prayer and affirmation into concrete action during the course of your day. The action can derive from an insight, a new way of looking at things, or a desire to change your consciousness, but, ideally, it will manifest in some way in words or deeds or both.

### Readings

*Ephesians 4:23: Be constantly renewed in the spirit of your mind, having a fresh mental and spiritual attitude putting on the new nature which is created in God's image.*

*Romans 12:2: Be transformed by the renewing of your thinking and your attitudes.*

### Reflection

*In nature, one sees the transformation of the caterpillar into the butterfly, but is this possible for humans? Can our "nature" be so changed that people find it difficult to recognize us? Yet I know*

*some people to whom this has happened. To me,
they are not who they used to be, but are now
much happier and more peaceful. So I would have
to acknowledge that change is possible, even
though I don't understand how it works.*

## Prayer

*Holy Spirit, you are the sacred transformer of our
nature. You are our spiritual therapist who causes
the change to take place where it really counts, in
our inner being. I give you, Holy Spirit, full permission to help me rise above the caterpillar stage
to the butterfly stage. Come, Holy Spirit.*

## Affirmation

*The Holy Spirit is at work in me now, renewing
me, reviving me, transforming me into the elegant
spirit I was created to be.*

## Action Step

*Work on your attitudes today by observing others'
attitudes without judgment, and then decide
which image you desire to portray—positive or negative, joyful or sad, strong or weak, complaining or
uplifting. The choice is yours.*

---

[1] For further study of the Lord's Prayer, see my tape set, *The Lord's
Prayer (from the Aramaic),* as well as the works of Neil Douglas-Klotz,
especially *Prayers of the Cosmos* and *The Hidden Gospel: Decoding the
Spiritual Message of the Aramaic Jesus.*

# Chapter Six

⌘

# Prayer, the Holy Spirit, and Healing

*T*he Acts of the Apostles (2:42) says of the first followers of the apostles, "They devoted themselves to the
apostles' teaching and fellowship, to the breaking of
bread and the prayers." Nothing ever got in the way of the
early followers going to the apostles' teaching sessions. The
result of their devotion is apparent in the very next verse:
"Everyone was filled with awe, and many signs and wonders were done by the apostles." This was not a part-time
awareness, as the text makes clear. "Every day they continued together in the temples and, breaking bread in their
homes, they ate together with glad and sincere hearts, prais-
ing God and enjoying the favor of all of the people."

When folks ask me how they can get their loved ones to
love God and be open to the loving and transforming energy
of Holy Spirit, I say, "Show them your life." If you want your
loved ones to change, *you* change, because that's what they'll
be looking at. If you go to a church, synagogue, mosque, temple, meditation session, yoga weekend, or healing workshop,
but you come back unchanged and continue with the same negative attitude and unloving behavior, the people in your life
won't see any reason to change themselves. When Jesus said,
"Let your light shine forth," he was saying that we should be
enthusiastic in showing the presence of the Spirit within us.

But to be able to show that *enthusiasm* (a word whose root

meaning is to be "filled with God"), we need to charge our energy cells through prayer. Prayer with the understanding of the Christ energy—the energy of Love that filled Jesus when he was on the earth and that is still available to us today— makes the gifts and the fruit of the Spirit come alive in our lives. That kind of prayer allows the Holy Spirit to manifest in and through us. It brings us health, healing, wholeness, and prosperity; it also brings us love, fills up our emptiness and loneliness, and gives us peace of mind and a joyful heart.

But what does it mean to pray with the understanding of the Christ energy? This is what happened at that first Pentecost, when the 120 men and women of the fledgling spiritual community gathered and prayed in the Spirit of Jesus. I believe they were primarily meditating on the presence of Jesus and thinking about the personality of Jesus. Indeed, for the first couple of centuries after Jesus left the earth, the early church concentrated on his name, which represents his persona. The Book of Acts says, in essence, "They stepped out in the name of Jesus, they preached in the name of Jesus, they spoke in the name of Jesus, they taught in the name of Jesus, they healed in the name of Jesus, they did miracles in the name of Jesus." However, that doesn't mean that they danced around saying, "Jesus, Jesus, Jesus" all the time. It means that they let the Holy Spirit within them shine forth through one of the strongest, most powerful prayers anyone can pray: the name of their master followed by silence.

When the early church gathered in fellowship, they probably sang songs of praise and then became still. In one moment of such stillness, at the first Christian Pentecost, a powerful light like a flame came above their heads, a symbol of purification, inner healing, forgiveness, reconciliation. And then that light activated the spirit of God within them until they were literally what St. Paul later called "aglow with the Spirit."

Of all the disciples described in the Gospels and the Acts,

the one who was the most completely transformed is the same one Jesus picked as leader: Peter. When you read chapter 18 of the Gospel of John, you find a man named Simon who is impetuous, rather fearful, anxious, and tense. By the time you encounter him again in the second and third chapters of the Book of Acts, you discover an entirely different person. Something has happened besides the change in his name from Simon to Peter. That something was prayer that led to his being infused with the Spirit. After that great Pentecostal experience came upon him, he was no longer afraid. He stepped out in front of all of the people who he knew could kill him and spoke to them in bold language. According to Acts, because of that movement of the Holy Spirit, 3,000 people followed the teachings of Jesus that day.

Conventional Christians might say that Peter got a good dose of the Holy Spirit, but that's not the whole story, for while the Holy Spirit was given to him, Peter also *accepted* the Holy Spirit. We have the same opportunity, but we often quench the Holy Spirit by saying no or not understanding what's happening. We may sense that to say yes means we will have to die to ourselves, that doing as the Holy Spirit guides may mean doing things we do not want to do. And yet you can't have health and healing and all of the other good things life has to offer without the help of the Holy Spirit.

In the Gospel of John (14:15ff), Jesus says, "I am going to send you another helper who is going to take my place." What Jesus is saying is that God will give you wisdom and understanding just as if he were there in the flesh with you, because in a sense he will be. The Holy Spirit will guide and direct you. When you sit down to pray with this understanding, you will feel the living waters beginning to stir and well up within you and move throughout your whole being.

At the beginning of Acts, which takes up where the Gospels leave off, Jesus is talking to the apostles, telling them that they will receive the power of the Holy Spirit. He tells them to be his witnesses in Judea and throughout the world, and then, according to the Scripture, he rises up into the sky. The apostles seem dumbstruck, just standing there watching. Undoubtedly they stood there a long time, until two men in white robes who seem to be angelic messengers appear by the apostles and say to them, in effect, "Hey, you guys, stop looking into the sky and get to work."

Like so many of us, the first apostles stood around doing nothing. We say we want enlightenment, we want to learn to be more compassionate or to heal an ailment, but we worry what our spouse or friends might think if we take action. So we throw water on the flame of the Holy Spirit. The New Testament says that children of God are led by the Spirit of God. It's not enough to be Spirit-filled; we have to be Spirit-led. We can't just stare at the skies wondering where the guru went; we have to get on with the work of God, living by the inspiration coming from within.

In his Letter to the Ephesians (5:18-19), Paul writes, "Do not get drunk with wine, for that is debauchery; but be filled with the Spirit, addressing one another in psalms and hymns and spiritual songs, singing and making melody to the Lord with all your heart." In the original Greek, the verb translated into English as "be filled" is once again a continuous form meaning "go on being filled." To "be filled with the Holy Spirit" implies that it's a one-shot affair, like being born again, whereas the author intended to mean, "Go on being filled until the day you die. Go on being filled with the Giver and then give to others."

I speak from experience when I say that all of us have been taught a kind of false piety that is pointless. One time an Assembly of God minister asked me if I would preach in his church on a Wednesday night because he had to be away. I agreed and led the service, and about a week later the minister came to me and said, "By the way, Ron, this is for helping me that Wednesday night." He handed me a check for $75.

"Oh, Bill," I said, "you really don't have to do that."

"Oh," he said, "yes I do."

"No, no, here," I said, handing the check back to him.

"No," he said. "You take that."

"Well, I really shouldn't."

"Let me tell you something," Bill said. "You did a service for God. Now it's as if God Himself were giving you this gift, and by returning it to God, you are slapping Him in the face. Is that what you want to do?"

I took the $75 with a thankful heart, and I've been accepting gifts ever since.

The Holy Spirit is the source of all guidance, the source of power and wisdom for those who want it. Acts 1:8 reads, "You shall receive power when the Holy Spirit has come upon you." The Greek word for *power* is *dunamis,* from which we get our word *dynamite.* That's the kind of power the Holy Spirit gives us if we're open to it. So I watch for guidance from the Holy Spirit as She directs me efficiently and effectively toward the accomplishment of those goals and dreams.

The more you experience the Holy Spirit, the more *dunamis* you will receive. St. Peter received courage and power from the Spirit, and in Acts 3, we see the results in Peter's first healing. Peter and John are going to the temple at the hour of prayer—not surprising—when they encounter a man lame from birth. The man is doing about the only thing disabled people could do to survive in those days, which is to beg for alms. When he asks Peter and John for money, Peter directs his gaze at the man and says, "Look at us." You can easily imagine this as a scene out of a modern city, as you're being approached by a homeless person and asked for money. The homeless need money, sure, but they also need to be recognized and engaged on a human level. If instead of either turning away in disdain or digging into your pockets out of duty, you *talk* to someone who approaches you on the street asking for money, it can take the whole encounter to a different level.

Peter does just that. He tells the man to look at him and John.

"Silver and gold I have none," he then says, "but what I do have I give you. In the name of Jesus of Nazareth, stand up and walk."

He is saying, in effect, "Through the power and authority that I receive from my teacher, with his understanding of the healing presence within us, I command you to stand up and walk."

Nor does Peter give the man any time to think about what is happening or to remember that he actually wants money. Instead, he reaches down and pulls him by the hand and jerks him onto his feet. The man has no choice but to get up and be healed.

### What Is Spiritual Healing?

Spiritual healing is not about fighting illness, but releasing the power of the Holy Spirit, as Peter did with the man lame from birth. This concept is at the heart of a story told about Guglielmo Marconi, the inventor of the wireless. Until I heard this account, I was under the impression that Marconi was the only scientist trying to discover the wireless, but in fact, numerous scientists had set out to invent a wireless transmitter at around the same time. Marconi insisted that he would be the first. When questioned about how he knew this, Marconi said that all the other scientists were trying to study the resistance in the atmosphere to the transmission of words. "I have already discovered that there is no resistance," he said. He wasn't fighting some imaginary resistance, but was looking for a way to release the power that was already present.

Along those same lines, I have often wondered exactly what Jesus meant when he said, "Do not resist evil." The moment the subconscious accepts the thought that you could be getting sick and begins to fret about it—worry being

perhaps the most common form of resistance—you often *do* get sick. If you expect that you *won't* get a job, and think only about what will happen if you fail, then all of your energy will be put into *not getting* the job. If someone slaps you on the right cheek, Jesus said, pretend it never happened and give him the left. If someone demands you walk with them a mile, walk with him two. How can you do this? The answer is, you can't, without the energy of the Holy Spirit. Let go of your thoughts of illness and sickness, let go of the hurts of the past, let go of your broken relationships and your so-called erroneous thoughts. The moment you do, the stirring of the Holy Spirit will begin to well up within you and you will sense a peace and joy you cannot experience until you begin to let go of all of the negatives.

Sometimes you know you must forgive but have a hard time doing so. What helps me get started on the forgiveness path is to picture Jesus with his hands out in front of him, palms up. Then I see myself writing down the name of the person or situation that's bothering me, and I mentally put it into Jesus' hands. The moment that name or problem hits his hands, the brilliant light of the Spirit comes forth and burns it up. *It's gone.* You can do the same thing, substituting another sacred being for Jesus if that feels more comfortable. Anytime the thought of the problematical person or situation starts to come back, use your mind and repeat, "I bless you with the love of Jesus. Jesus is taking care of the situation now. Thank you, Jesus."

Our main focus should not be to fight the so-called evil in the world, but to discover ways to release the good. Spiritual healing means unblocking the Spirit to flow through our lives, changing and transforming us. Spiritual healing is learning to live in the Holy Spirit of wholeness. Spiritual healing is releasing the potential life of the Divine that is always present within us. But we still have to *act* on that potential.

In spiritual healing as well as in conventional medicine,

the best course is to deal with the principles of healing when you're well. Don't wait until you get sick. If you spend all your time focused on the material world and keep putting off creating space for a spiritual practice, for daily prayer and meditation, and for adhering to the principles I've outlined, you can't expect results to happen overnight once you're ill. That would be like a ballplayer not working out in the off-season, skipping spring training and exhibition games, and expecting to join the team on opening day and play flawless baseball. It won't happen. Once you become ill, your mental faculties and emotional stamina are already being taxed. You're likely to feel panic or depression or both when an illness sets in, and it can be a great comfort if you already have a spiritual routine in place and understand what you need to do to heal yourself. So I heartily recommend that you practice preventive spiritual medicine.

Above all, practicing preventive spiritual medicine means taking responsibility for your life. Don't fix your mind on your physical malady, especially when praying. Instead, fix your thoughts on God and wholeness and the plan that God has for you. We can't blame God anymore. The fundamental process of healing prayer is waking up to who we really are, keeping in mind the words of Jesus that the truth will set you free. The real meaning of the story of the Prodigal Son, which I discussed at length in *Prayer and the Five Stages of Healing*, is that the son ran away from who he really was. In the extended metaphor of that story, the Father represents the God-self within each of us, and that's what the boy was fleeing when he asked for his inheritance. He wanted to live in material consciousness, and so he squandered his inheritance on wild living. Jesus didn't elaborate, but you can be sure his audience knew what he was talking about. One line in the parable says, when the boy has fallen on hard times after blowing his bankroll, "He came back to his senses." That means he came back to the Father who lives within us all. When that

Father releases the Spirit in our lives and we're aware of it, we can party in the true sense of the word. We can celebrate life in the Spirit of the Christ.

"I am not here on my own, but He who sent me is true," Jesus said. "You do not know Him, but I know Him because I am from Him and He sent me" (John 7:28-29). That's a very modest way of saying, "I have to get out of the way and let the Divine process flow." Whenever I give a healing service, it is not totally spontaneous; I invest a lot of time preparing and planning. The Holy Spirit gives me the guidance as to what songs we will sing, what theme we will focus on, and what points to get across to the people. When the intuitive awareness comes to me to call out sicknesses that are being healed, it must be Holy Spirit and it must come at the precise moment that the Holy Spirit urges me to speak. So the words I speak are not really my words, but the words of the Spirit of God within me.

Sometimes you may feel the need to ask somebody to pray with you, perhaps because you can't handle a given situation. That's fine, but be alert to their language and attitude. The moment they start to sympathize with you and say, "Oh, dear, that's too bad," find somebody else to pray with. They're putting energy into negativity rather than reinforcing the positive attitude you need to heal yourself. Whereas if you tell someone you've just gotten a troubling diagnosis from the doctor, they may respond, "Good, let's pray." That person isn't saying it's good that you have a disease, but is focusing on the need to pray. Their attitude—as yours should be, if the roles are reversed—is "You be still. I'll speak." Then the person praying with you goes down deep to the Holy Spirit and waits for the Spirit to speak the words. Those words might be something based on the Scriptures, such as, "I love you with an everlasting love. Be not afraid. Let not your heart be troubled. I am with you. I will never forsake you. The light of God surrounds you. The love that will never forsake you is in you now. It's being released, overcoming all your fears and doubts. The Divine Spirit is with you." That kind of prayer moves mountains, and it moves people into healthy thinking. Here are some basic principles and suggestions for initiating the healing process through prayer:

— **Get centered and get a sense of oneness.** Because I am a follower of Jesus, my way of centering is to focus on a large statue of the Sacred Heart I have in my home, but you might just as easily use a crucifix or the statue of Quanyin, the Chinese goddess of mercy and compassion. I may also pick up a Scripture passage or spiritual book and open it until a sentence suddenly grabs me. Recently I was reading a book about the great spiritual healer Kathryn Kuhlman, when I came across a quote from Paul's Letter to the Colossians (1:29): "This is my work and I can do it only because Christ's mighty energy is at work in me." I put down the book, and the Holy Spirit began to bring thoughts and images to my mind of laying hands on the sick. A light started welling up within me and filled me with the desire to share that light of God's power and healing with others. Fifteen or twenty minutes went by, and I hardly noticed it. That's a powerful form of meditative prayer.

When you use a sacred image, forget the image itself and think about what it represents—love, peace, and joy. You don't have to say anything. Getting centered means focusing on love. After a while, the image may disappear and a brilliant light will come. I can sense that light with myself right in the center of it until I can't see myself anymore. When you get to that point and sense the peace of God flowing through you, that's the time to lay your hands on yourself if you're sick. It's also the time to lay your hands on someone else if they're sick, because the power in your hand is no longer you. It's the power of God flowing through you. There's nothing to get egotistical about. You're so absorbed by the light of God within you that you're not thinking of a need, you're not thinking of sickness, poverty, or unemployment. You're thinking only of God, Who is your source of health and everything else.

After such a meditation, you may get a little hunch, an idea to make a phone call, write a letter, or visit someone. I've learned that even if it's the most outlandish thing, I should follow through on it. Every time I do, a door opens—but I have to *do* something first. I have to pray, I have to meditate, I have to listen. After I speak, I have to shut up and listen, which is the hard part. And in that listening, if I hear the voice of the Spirit of God, I don't make excuses anymore. Once you do that, the enthusiasm and the zest for living begin to drain out of you as if someone has punctured your balloon. You've quenched the Holy Spirit, and the power goes right back within and waits for your obedience before it will emerge again. It's simple if you know the plan of action, and that's the plan of action that works for me.

Out of this oneness where there is no thought or need, listen to the flow of spiritual ideas. Remember the quote from the Book of Acts: "We live, move, and have our very being in the Holy Spirit." As we step aside and let the Spirit flow as we make contact in prayer and meditation, our lives are guided toward fulfillment and wholeness.

**— Healing is becoming aware of the life within us and then coming to the place where we celebrate that life within us.** John the Baptist said, "I must decrease, he must increase." *Translation:* The ego must diminish so that the great I Am, the Holy Spirit within me, can assume a larger role.

**— The more we let go, the more aware of God's presence we become.** Out of this conscious awareness comes direction, guidance, creative ideas, a flow of life, God, love, peace—all you could desire and more.

**— The starting point for healing is to make peace first with whatever condition you have.** Bless it, and let it go from your thoughts. Everything we do to help others should be motivated by the desire to help them and ourselves seek oneness with God.

# Chapter Seven

༄ ࿐

## Healing the Sick: Some Tried-and-True Techniques

O ver the years, I've learned to rely on a number of techniques associated with prayer and healing that have
a long tradition behind them. But some people tend
to write off these approaches precisely because they're old or
traditional—just as many modern spiritually inclined people
from Catholic backgrounds rebel against traditionally Catholic
prayer forms such as the rosary. People often ask me, for
instance, why visualization is so important in prayer. When
you imagine a goal that would help raise your self-esteem,
and you close your eyes and visualize the accomplishment
of that goal, you'll feel an awakening of the Spirit in you. An
emotion begins to build that all of a sudden reaches your
mind and says, "I can do that." That is faith, and faith goes
hand-in-hand with the picture in your mind, good or bad.
When you believe that picture in your mind, something starts
happening based on whether it's a positive or negative image.
That's why we want to learn to reprogram our thoughts to
picture good, to picture light and Divine energy—the Holy
Spirit in the midst of our lives.

For this reason, when I say the Our Father, I try to see it
in images. When I say "Our Father," for instance, I picture a
daddy who's smiling and radiantly alive. He has outstretched
arms and I'm just a little child, and I run into his arms and
He pulls me up on His lap and cuddles me close to His heart.

"Our daddy who is unlimited, anything is possible to you." And when I begin saying an expanded version of that prayer, "Our Father/Mother, everywhere in the universe," I can also picture a loving Mother, a Goddess of great tenderness and maternal warmth who enfolds me in Her arms. So take your pick, but do use images as much as possible when you pray, especially if you're a beginner. If you pray without those images, you might quench the Holy Spirit, throwing water on the radiant flame. Over time, as you develop a greater facility with prayer and meditation, you may need to rely less on specific visual images.

### Signs and Wonders

Laying on of hands is another ancient technique that goes back to the founding of Christianity, but which can take surprisingly different forms today. When I was at a conference at Notre Dame, a number of people in a prayer group from Mexico came to give witness to what God was doing in their lives. One man in his late 20s got up to tell how he came to God. He said that most of his life from his teenage years on, he was a drunk. He would come home and beat his wife while their five-year-old daughter watched in horror. This went on for a couple of years until the wife started going to the prayer meetings that were being held in a Mexican border town. At one point, she decided to take their little girl with her. As they were praying, the girl was getting excited, because she really believed everything the spiritual teacher was saying about prayer and healing—that, for instance, nothing is impossible for God. She told her mother, "Well, then, with Daddy, it's not impossible. He can change."

So the girl went home armed with an awareness of the Holy Spirit and sat up with her mother until Daddy came home in one of his drunken rages. He went through the house screaming and yelling, but the little girl didn't become petrified, anxious, or tense. She walked up and touched him on the knee—because she wasn't any taller than that—and said, "Be healed." The man went down "under the power," swooning and falling to the floor in a kind of trance. He came up, and by his own witness, he never touched alcohol again, and turned back to God.

The Book of Acts (19:11) says, "God did extraordinary miracles through Paul. Handkerchiefs and aprons that had touched him were taken to the sick and their illnesses were cured." Based on that, I have long used prayer cloths as a technology for healing. These are blessed cloths that you can hold to whatever part of the body is afflicted. The blessing on the cloths acts as a kind of laying on of hands at a distance, and these cloths have helped effect some remarkable healings among people I have ministered to.

Most of all, when healing, be creative. If someone calls you to pray with her and you don't know exactly what to do, take a deep breath and recall the phrase, "I am God breathed" (as described in the exercise in chapter 3), until you sense a welling up of joy accompanied by confidence in that truth. Then as you visualize in your mind a light going through that part of the body that is diseased, sense what happens within your being. The resultant sensations of peace and tranquility will tell you that you have the faith now to move mountains. Then, just place the cloth on yourself or whoever you are praying for, and focus only on God, not the cloth. Remember the words of the prophet Zachariah: "It is not by your might, not by your power, but by my Spirit, says the Lord."

One last powerful prayer tool that will assist you in healing is reading and meditating on the word of God. You may be thinking, *Oh, I already read the Scriptures on occasion. What is that going to do?* One night when I was still a Catholic priest, I didn't know exactly what I was to preach or teach about at a healing service. I had with me the paraphrase of Scripture known as the Living Bible, because it is easy to read and makes the Scriptures more accessible. I was sitting on the bed thinking about what I should do when I said, "Lord, you're just going to have to show me. Give me a word that will inspire me or uplift me." It's difficult to go before people with your knees knocking together when you're not exactly sure what you're supposed to do. I opened up the Bible to Luke 17:6, and read, "If your faith were only the size of a mustard seed, Jesus answered, you could say to this mulberry tree, 'Be uprooted and planted in the sea,' and it would obey you." That sentence spoke to me, because it was saying, in effect, "Your command would bring immediate results." I felt a welling up of power within me, and I picked myself up off that chair, went into the chapel, and buzzed across to that pulpit as if I were floating.

As I led the worship and the praise, waiting for the moment in which I was to preach, that Scripture verse kept echoing in my ear. Call it a command or a prayer of affirmation (as discussed in chapter 2). When it came time to preach, I told the congregation, "The Spirit wants me to heal even before I preach, because the kingdom of God is upon us." I can remember that night as if it were yesterday. Twenty-three people came forward and lined up, the first night I ever did that. I asked everyone to join me in singing, and then I went down the aisle and touched every one of them and said, "Be healed. Be healed." Three or four of the men went down under the power, which had never happened at my service before. I thought I had pushed them, but I wasn't sure. They landed on the floor, and I didn't know what was going on. Then one lady started weeping and swinging her arm around. "What's the problem?" I asked.

"There's no problem," she said. "I was in an automobile accident 20 years ago, and ever since, I haven't been able to get my arm any higher than this." She raised it up to her shoulder. "When you touched me, it was like an electric shock went through me and my arm bolted straight up into the air."

Afterwards, I learned from talking to the people who were there that night, suffering from everything from that frozen arm to deafness, that 22 out of the 23 were healed. That showed me the importance of reading and meditating on the word of God.

### God's Complementary Medicine

— **Positive faith is an attitude.** St. James reminds us in his Letter, however, that without action, faith is dead. Unless you step out in that faith and take a risk, it's not really faith. All through the Book of Acts, we hear about the apostles' "faith in that name." But as we've seen, when they preached in the name of Jesus, taught in the name of Jesus, or healed in the name of Jesus, that doesn't mean they repeated his name over and over—and neither should we. That will get you nowhere. We have to realize that the name signifies the person of Jesus and the understanding he had of himself, as well as a knowledge of his mission. When the disciples did something "in the name of Jesus," they did it just as Jesus would do it, just as Jesus told them how. And the same holds true for us. It's as if Jesus himself were in our shoes, doing something through us, no matter what our religion may be. Peter wondered why the people were so astounded that a healing occurred. "You thought it happened because of our piety and holiness?" he asked rhetorically. The reason the man was healed, he explained, was that the apostles trusted in the teaching authority of Jesus and trusted what Jesus told them they could do.

— **Anointing with oil.** Oil is symbolic of the Holy Spirit, but in the early days, it was more than a mere symbol. When the disciples went off to anoint the sick, they didn't just make the sign of the cross on someone's forehead with a thumb dipped in oil; they laid it on thick, because it was considered a healing ointment to be rubbed on in much the same way that today we rub on Vicks VapoRub. They might even have given the ailing person a rubdown with the oil. Anointing with oil today can mean laying both hands on a person, and then taking the oil and rubbing the back or chest with it.[1]

— **Intercessory Prayer**. Most people think that intercessory prayer means begging and pleading for another individual. But if you were praying that way for me, I would say please don't bother, because your prayer isn't going to get any higher than your forehead. "Intercessor" means "one who passes between," or one who stands in the gap. A person in need of healing is often too depressed, maybe even too sick, to pray with conviction and feeling. What they don't need is another sick person with sick attitudes to come and stand in the gap. They need people who understand and use the power of command and affirmation, who can visualize the presence of God because they know God. They need people who are able, like Jesus, to say, "Lord, I know you hear my prayer and answer it," or "Lazarus, come forth." Intercessory prayer means that you're standing in the gap for an ailing person, decreeing a positive result.

In the Old Testament book of Exodus (17:8-13), Moses told Joshua to fight a battle and said, "Tomorrow I will stand on the top of the hill with the rod of God in my hand." I don't know how the authors of the Torah would have characterized the rod or staff used by Moses to get water from the rock at Horeb, among other wonders, but I see it symbolically as Moses' awareness of his power and authority. During the battle that ensued between Joshua and Amalek, Moses stood on the hill along with Aaron and Hur, and as long as Moses held aloft the rod of God, the Israelites prevailed, but when his arms tired and he lowered them, Amalek prevailed. If you've ever tried holding your arms out straight, you know you can't do it for very long. So Aaron and Hur placed a stone for Moses to sit on and, standing on either side of him, each of them held up one of his hands until Joshua prevailed. The message is clear to me: In order to prevail, Moses needed help, and he got it from two strong individuals, not by begging and pleading with God, but by simple decree.

My favorite story with respect to faith and healing, though, comes from the Old Testament Book known as 2 Kings, Chapter 5. Naaman was commander of the Syrian army, "a valiant soldier but he had leprosy." As it happens, the Syrians had captured a young girl from Israel who became servant to Naaman's wife. The captive told her mistress that if only Naaman would go see the great prophet in Samaria, Elisha would cure him of his leprosy. Naaman got permission and left with money, cattle, and a letter of introduction to the King of Israel: "With this letter I'm sending my servant Naaman to you so that you may cure him of his leprosy." I'm not sure why the Syrian king sent Naaman to the King of Israel to be healed rather than to the prophet Elisha, but the result was nearly disastrous.

When the king read the letter, he tore his robes in anger at the Syrian's presumption that he could somehow cure Naaman. But Elisha heard about this and sent a message to the king offering his own services. So Naaman went to Elisha with all of his money, horses, and men, and when he got to Elisha's house, Elisha sent a messenger out to him telling him to go and wash himself seven times in the river Jordan and he would be healed.

But Naaman was insulted. "I thought that he would surely come out to me, and stand, and call upon the name of the Lord, his God, wave his hand over me and cure me of my leprosy." I can relate to that because so many people who come to my healing services get upset if I don't touch them. I'm trying to teach them that the Spirit of God is in them and in the very atmosphere around them so that they don't need to continue focusing on me, but they don't always get it.

Naaman even suggested that there were a couple of rivers in Syria better than the Jordan, and he steamed off in a huff. Naaman's servants went to him, however, and said, "If the prophet had told you to do some great thing, would you not have done it? How much more, then, when he tells you 'Wash and be cleansed'?" Remember that those who prove themselves in little matters will be called to greater things.

Naaman was no dummy. He realized that he had made a fool of himself—that God is not our servant but we are God's servants. So he went and dipped himself in the Jordan seven times as directed by Elisha, "and his flesh was restored and became clean like that of a young boy." Obedience to the Spirit of God yields positive results.

How well I know this. Anything great accomplished in my life happened because I was obedient. I'm no saint, but when I'm absolutely sure that God has spoken, I launch out in the direction the guidance leads me. When it looks impossible but I'm sure that God has spoken, I obey. I leave my comfort zone of mediocrity and step out in the zone of risk, and Spirit creates a miracle. That's all it takes. When we say, "Thy will be done," we must understand that the will of God is to give us the kingdom. We're commanding it to manifest, not asking God to manifest it for us.

Finally, let common sense play a role in your healing life, both for you and those around you. If you smoke, give it up. Don't drink to excess. Follow a nutritionally sound diet—not a fad or crash diet, but something you can live with every day. Get enough exercise to keep your cardiovascular system healthy without risking serious injury. Above all, be humbly open and receptive to the guidance of the Holy Spirit at all times.

---

[1] For further understanding of these techniques and of the symbols of the Holy Spirit, refer to my book *Holy Spirit: The Boundless Energy of God*.

# Chapter Eight

ᢍ ᢍ

## Healing in Sacred Scripture

*"He sent forth His word and healed them."*
Psalm 107:20

*I*s there power in the word of God? The Book of Genesis opens up with the statement that God said let there be, and it was. Jesus said that if you have faith to believe, you can speak to your mountain, and as long as you're speaking in the Holy Spirit, you're going to move that mountain. Nothing shall be impossible to you; nothing shall stand in your way.

But the written word in the form of the world's great Scriptures also has the power to heal you. As I said earlier, if you have a specific physical problem, say, paralysis, look for a passage in the Scriptures where a paralytic is healed. If you have a problem with blindness or you're losing your sight, look for a passage in the Scripture where this particular ailment is cured. If you're having difficulty with your hearing, look to where a deaf person is healed, and ponder that story. Read it and then close your eyes and meditate on it until you're the paralytic, the blind person, the deaf person being healed. And whatever occurs in the course of that passage, visualize it being done to you. Then remember to end your prayer with the spoken word "Amen," which means "So be it. It is so. I believe." (Consult the chart of healings and relevant Scripture passages for easy reference.)

## Some References to Healings in the Gospels

| HEALINGS BY JESUS | MATT. | MARK | LUKE | JOHN |
|---|---|---|---|---|
| The nobleman's son | | | | 4:46-54 |
| The man with an unclean spirit | | 1:21-28 | 4:31-37 | |
| Simon's mother-in-law | 8:14-15 | 1:29-31 | 4:38-39 | |
| A leper | 8:1-4 | 1:40-45 | 5:12-16 | |
| Paralytic carried by four men | 9:1-8 | 2:1-12 | 5:17-26 | |
| Sick man at pool of Bethesda | | | | 5:2-18 |
| The man with withered hand | 12:9-14 | 3:1-6 | 6:6-11 | |
| The centurion's servant | 8:5-13 | | 7:2 -10 | |
| Raising of the widow's son | | | 7:11-17 | |
| The demoniac(s) at Gadara | 8:28-34 | 5:1-20 | 8:26-35 | |
| Woman with an issue of blood | 9:20-22 | 5:25-34 | 8:43-48 | |
| Raising of Jairus's daughter | 9:18-26 | 5:21-43 | 8:40-56 | |
| Two blind men indoors | 9:27-31 | | | |
| Daughter of Canaanite woman | 15:21-28 | 7:24-30 | | |
| Deaf man w/speech impediment | | 7:32-37 | | |
| Blind man at Bethsaida | | 8:22-26 | | |
| Epileptic boy | 17:14-21 | 9:14-19 | 9:37-43 | |
| Man born blind (Siloam) | | | | 9:1-14 |
| Woman bent double | | | 13:10-17 | |
| The man with dropsy | | | 14:1-6 | |
| Raising of Lazarus | | | | 11:1-44 |
| Blind Bartimaeus | 20:29-34 | 10:46-52 | 18:35-43 | |
| Malchus's ear | | | 22:50-51 | |
| Crowd at Peter's door | 8:16-17 | 1:32 -34 | 4:40-41 | |
| Crowds, after the healing of leper | | | 5:14-16 | |
| The crowd near Capernaum | 12:15-21 | 3: 7-12 | 6:17-19 | |
| Sick people healed, after | | | | |
|     John the Baptist's question | 11:2-6 | | | |
| The blind and lame in Temple | 21:14 | | | |
| Some sick people at Nazareth | 13:53-58 | 6:16 | | |

# The Healing Ministry of Others

| | MATT. | MARK | LUKE | ACTS |
|---|---|---|---|---|
| Jesus' ministry described | 11:2-6 | | 7:18-21A | |
| The twelve sent | 10:l-11:1 | 3:13-19 | 9:1-11 | |
| The seventy sent | | | 10:1-24 | |
| Disciples attempt to cast out demons | 17:14-21 | 9:14-29 | 9:37-45 | |
| Power to bind and loose | 16:13-20 | 8:27-30 | 9:18-22 | |
| Great commission | 28:16-20 | 6:14-20 | 24:44-53 | 1:1-11 |
| Jesus' ministry described | | | | 2:22 |
| Signs and wonders at apostles' hands | | | | 2:42-47 |
| Healing of lame beggar | | | | 3:1-4:22 |
| Prayer for confidence and healing signs | | | | 4:23-31 |
| Signs and wonders at apostles' hands | | | | 5:12-16 |
| Ministry of Stephen | | | | 6:8-15 |
| Ministry of Philip | | | | 8:4-13 |
| Ananias and Saul | | | | 9:4-10–19 |
| Peter heals Aeneas (Lydda) | | | | 9:32-35 |
| Peter heals Dorcas (Joppa) | | | | 9:36-43 |
| The ministry of Jesus | | | | 10:34-41 |
| Magician struck blind by Paul | | | | 13:4-12 |
| Paul and Barnabas in Iconium | | | | 14:1-7 |
| Lame man at Lystra | | | | 14:8-18 |
| Paul raised at Lystra | | | | 14:19-20 |
| Slave girl at Philippi | | | | 16:16-40 |
| Paul at Ephesus | | | | 19:8-20 |
| Eutychus raised from the dead | | | | 20:7-12 |
| Paul recalls Ananias | | | | 22:12-21 |

Lest anyone get the wrong impression, I don't believe that the Christian Scriptures are the only source of healing power. As the Indian holy book known as the *Rig Veda* says, "Truth is one, but sages call it by different names." An article in the *New York Times* in 1998 tells about the healing services of Sheikh Abdel Aziz ibn Ali of Sudan. A Sufi master who is often at odds with the hard-line Islamic government of Sudan, Sheikh Abdel Aziz heals people by reciting verses from the Quran. The *Times* reporter interviewed a number of people who had been cured of migraines, blindness, and other ailments. "I do the same things that doctors do," Abdel Aziz is quoted as saying. "For this the doctors have become angry with me and they have complained to the Government. That is why they try to stop me." According to the article, Abdel Aziz often preaches up to four times a day, and more than 800 people attend most sessions.

Like most genuine healers, the Sheik declines to accept responsibility for healing people. He claims that he's doing nothing more than reciting the sacred words the Prophet Muhammad received from Allah, the Arabic name for God. Allah, says Abdel Aziz, does the rest.

I recommend owning more than one version of the Bible, incidentally, as well as copies of the sacred Scriptures of other religious traditions, such as the *Upanishads* and the *Bhagavad-Gita* from the Hindu tradition; the *Dhammapada*, or sayings of the Buddha; the Quran; the Talmud (commentaries on the Torah, or first five books of the Hebrew Scripture); the *Tao Te Ching*, and other works.[1] Whenever you read the Christian Scriptures, read the same passage in several different Bibles to get a fuller meaning from the various translations. Then sit back in the presence of the Holy Spirit, and open your heart for the Spirit to reveal the truth to you about those particular passages. When you do that, you slowly but surely begin to be transformed into the power of that word.

It's like a seed. Today you see a mound of dirt; tomorrow there's a stalk with tomatoes on it. The next day, those tomatoes are in the market, and then they're on your plate. You do not become the tomato when you eat it; it becomes you. It goes into your system, into your body and blood, and develops your cells. Likewise, when you devour the sacred writings of the world and meditate on them in silence, allowing the Holy Spirit to do the work, you begin to digest them until you absorb the words into your system, and you and God become one.

Hindus, Buddhists, and Taoists alike believe that mantras formed from certain sacred syllables also have the power to heal us emotionally, physically, and spiritually. All the world's Scriptures contain beautiful images and inspirational words that have the power to heal us by imparting life-giving strength and wisdom. Let me give you an example of what I mean by that, returning to the Scriptures I know best. The beautiful picture that is given in Genesis of the creation of the world begins with a dark void. Nothing had been created, and hovering over the darkness was the Holy Spirit waiting to create. The text says, "The Spirit of God was moving over the face of the waters." The Hebrew word *ruach* means both "spirit" and "wind," so that line has also been translated, "A Divine wind was moving over the waters." That's significant because the Greek word used in the New Testament to refer to the Holy Spirit, *pneuma*, also means both "spirit" and "wind" (and, like *ruach*, is feminine in gender). When God spoke the words "Let there be," the Holy Spirit began to move and bring the world into creation.

Think now what's available for you when you speak the positive, grace-filled, power-filled words that Jesus spoke. Think for a moment what would happen to your life if you sat down and began to say the same words that Jesus said, and began to let the Spirit hovering within take those words and create a power source inside of you. As you put your hands on your body, think of the words of Jesus, "Be healed. Be made whole."

## Exercise: Preparing for Healing Prayer— What You Can Do

1.  Recognize and ponder these three important truths:

    A.  God is love, and this is the powerful energy that heals with no strings attached.

    B.  God loves you unconditionally, for you are the "child" of our heavenly Father/Mother—you are the beloved one. Learn to accept that by pondering this truth daily, especially for ten minutes upon rising and ten minutes prior to retiring at night: "I am God's beloved child."

    C.  God desires to heal us, restore us, and bless us abundantly because God's nature is pure goodness.

2.  What can you do to release God's Divine healing energy (Holy Spirit) from within for your wholeness?

    A.  Admit that you need help. That is, be honest and humble with yourself.

    B.  Ask for help, especially healing prayer from others.

    C.  Pray for your own healing in a straightforward manner as many Biblical persons did:
        *Lord, that I may see*
        *Lord, that I may walk*
        *Lord, that I may be healed.*
        *Thank you.*

(Note: No begging or pleading, as this produces great amounts of fear energy.)

    D.  Seek out ways you can assist in your own healing by:

        • attending healing prayer gatherings.

- attending classes in spirituality and prayer.

- letting a loved one pray with you.

- reading and meditating on sacred Scripture.

- listening to audiotapes and/or watching videos dealing with the power of prayer and spirituality to heal.

- monitoring your thoughts, feelings, and behavior, being aware of any negative energies such as resentment, unforgiveness, and bitterness, desiring only to give, receive, and be love by letting go of negativities.

- associating with individuals and participating in gatherings (including religious gatherings) that uplift, stimulate, and validate you. Avoid those individuals and gatherings that deplete your energy and cause you to feel less than human.

- replacing fear thoughts with thoughts of love.

E.   Pray for others who are suffering.

F.   Develop an attitude of gratitude.

---

[1] For more information on the Scriptures of the world's great spiritual traditions, see *The Joy of Sects* by Peter Occhiogrosso.

# Chapter Nine

୶ ଚ

# The Ladder of the Beatitudes

After Jesus announced his arrival, so to speak, in the temple of Nazareth, where he had been brought up, proclaiming, "The Spirit of the Lord is upon me," the locals marveled and said, "Is this not Joseph's son?" It was a preeminently human response. Imagine that your next-door neighbor's daughter goes away to college, graduates, and a few years later becomes a popular spiritual teacher and healer who tours the country and attracts tens of thousands to her services. Then she comes to speak at the town hall where she grew up. People would probably say much the same thing. "Isn't she the girl who used to work at the Wendy's in town? What is she doing telling us how to live?" Jesus picks up on the locals' bemusement and skepticism. "Undoubtedly, you will quote to me the proverb 'Physician, heal thyself,'" he says with barely concealed irony. "'What we have heard you did in Capernaum, do here in your own country, too.'"

But he doesn't stop there. He's onto their all-too-human expectations, their miracle-baiting, as it were, and he's several leaps ahead of them. "Truly I say to you, no prophet is acceptable in his own country. But in truth I tell you, there were many widows in Israel in the days of Elijah, when the heaven was shut up three years and six months, when there came a great famine all over the land; and Elijah was sent to none of them but only to Zarephath, in the land of Sidon, to a woman who was a widow. And there were many lepers in Israel in the time of Elisha; and none of them was cleansed, but only Naaman the Syrian." Jesus was clearly well versed in Hebrew Scripture. Whether he studied with the rabbis, or on his own, or was instructed on the astral plane as some believe, is unimportant. In any case, he is certainly aware of the story of Naaman, which, as we have just seen, is crucial to our understanding of his own healing principles. Jesus is in rare form here, giving his Nazarene neighbors a lesson in irony, and they don't exactly warm to it.

"When they heard this," the text goes on, "all in the synagogue were filled with wrath." Jesus is a real hit from the get-go! He has barely started his public ministry, and he already has the hoi polloi up in arms. They're so incensed that they lead him to a cliff at the edge of town and are ready to pitch him off when he practices some kind of subtle mind control and escapes right through their midst. What a start to the preaching life—virtually run out of town on a rail!

Once Jesus gets loose of the confines of home and moves on to Capernaum (like many great American artists who flee the small towns of their childhood and head for the big cities), the folk there are "astonished at his teaching, for he spoke as one with authority." The modern translation might be, "He spoke like someone who had been there and lived to tell about it." In street parlance, you could say that Jesus walks his talk. And as if to prove it, he immediately heals a demoniac possessed of an unclean spirit. The crowd, now, goes wild.

Yet all this is just a warm-up to the main event. Jesus' first major teaching to the masses is generally reckoned to be the Sermon on the Mount, a long discourse that covered a multitude of subjects and in all likelihood took place over several days. First among his topics are the beatitudes, the Magna Carta of Jesus' teachings in the sense that they lay out his basic game plan. I prefer to think of them as the "be attitudes," because they delineate the attitudes of being immersed in the

Spirit of God—the beautiful attitudes of Christ consciousness. Jesus is teaching and proclaiming the attitudes that you cannot form from the outside but that must be formed from within through the power of the Holy Spirit. They appear in the Gospel of Matthew, chapter 5:

> *Now when he saw the crowds, he went up on a mountainside and sat down. His disciples came to him and he began to teach them saying:*
> *Blessed are the poor in spirit, for theirs is the kingdom of heaven.*
> *Blessed are those who mourn, for they shall be comforted.*
> *Blessed are the meek, for they will inherit the earth.*
> *Blessed are those who hunger and thirst for righteousness, for they will be filled.*
> *Blessed are the merciful, for they will be shown mercy.*
> *Blessed are the pure in heart, for they will see God.*
> *Blessed are the peace makers, for they will be called children of God.*
> *Blessed are those who are persecuted because of righteousness, for theirs is the kingdom of heaven.*
> *Blessed are you when people insult you, persecute you, and falsely say all kinds of evil against you because of me. Rejoice and be glad, because great is your reward in heaven. For in this same way, they persecuted the prophets who were before you.*

The beatitudes are not simple statements; they are exclamations. Sometimes we read them as a series of declarative sentences, but try saying them this way, for example: *How happy are those who know their need for God, because the kingdom of heaven is theirs!* What we translate as "blessed" could just as easily be translated as "fortunate" or "prosperous" or "happy," since it applies to people who know their need for God and trust in Him. They recognize His presence in their life.

"Blessed are those who mourn, for they shall be comforted" could more expressively be rendered, "How happy are those who know what sorrow means, for they will be given courage and comfort!" And instead of saying, "Blessed are the poor in spirit," we could say it this way: "Oh, the blessedness, the pure joy and awesome wonder of those who are humble!" To make matters worse, "Blessed are the poor in spirit" is often misinterpreted as "Blessed are the poor." That is not what that beatitude says. Nowhere in the Scriptures does God extol poverty, or what we might call "lack consciousness," as a good thing, because poverty breeds crime and corruption, injustice and lack of charity. When Jesus made his famous but misunderstood statement that "it is harder for a rich man to enter heaven than for a camel to fit through the eye of a needle," he was not saying that money is intrinsically evil. He was warning us not to put our *trust* in money and possessions, but in *God*. The poor in spirit could more descriptively be translated as "the humble, those who do not suffer from ego inflation, but trust in God."

As we saw earlier, the nuances in what Jesus said in Aramaic, which is a form of Hebrew, are often lost when translated into the Greek in which all the Gospels were written. Jesus said, for example, "How humble or how blessed are the *anawim*." The anawim were the Jewish people who trusted God completely—in other words, they were not attached to their possessions because they knew God would provide.

Jesus did not present the beatitudes as separate statements unrelated to each other, but as a stepladder. In order to get to the eighth step, which is the kingdom of heaven, you have to start with the first: humility. Once you're humble enough to realize your errors and mistakes, you'll become ready for the next step, which is to weep over them so that God's Spirit within you can be more fully released. When you're sorrowful, you'll be comforted. Did you ever notice that when you try to fight back your tears, you don't feel especially comforted or strengthened? You may think you are, but consider the possibility that you're avoiding your true feelings, thereby creating an energetic block on the inner plane.

Having cleansed yourself through humility and sorrow, you're ready to accept heavenly guidance and control. The third beatitude tells us that those who claim nothing—the meek—will be happy because the whole world will belong to them. If ever there was a dirty word in English, it has to be *meek*, for which modern synonyms include *wishy-washy* and *wimpy*. That's not what Jesus is talking about. In Greek, the word *meek* was used in the context of horse training. When they trained wild horses, they sought to "meek" them. They were not breaking the horse's spirit, but putting the horse under their control. In the *Upanishads,* we find the famous metaphor of the charioteer and the horses. The chariot that the ancient Aryans used to conquer India was propelled by one or more horses and usually carried two men—the one who held the reins and drove the chariot, and the one in back who shot the arrows and spears and did the killing. The chariot was a devastating killing machine against foot soldiers in those days, the Sherman tank of its era. But the Indian mystics turned the image around and applied its force to the conquest of human emotions and passions. Those passions are represented by the powerful horses; the charioteer's job is to control the horses and keep them from swerving off to one side or the other. If the horses go too fast, the warrior (or spiritual practitioner) will be thrown out of the chariot; if they go too slow, he will lose his effectiveness as a fighter (or adept).

What Jesus is saying is that the meek—those who can be trained to control their senses and passions—will inherit the earth. But you may wonder if such a thing has ever happened. Going back to the Indian tradition for a moment, think of Mahatma Gandhi. When everyone else saw only two options—fighting the enemy violently or giving in and being dominated and exploited—Gandhi told his people not to use the same methods as the oppressor. For a Hindu, Gandhi made an exceptionally good Christian! He once said that if Christians acted as if they really believed what Jesus taught, he would let them pour the water on his head to baptize him. In the end, Gandhi won freedom for his country by never lifting a knife or a gun, but by teaching people to control their passions and channel that energy for good.

According to the fourth beatitude, happy are those who are hungry and thirsty for true goodness, for they will be fully satisfied. Once you've subdued the senses—not by denying their existence or starving them, but by bringing them under your control—you can really begin to pursue the good life. Jesus is saying that you must want Truth so much that you feel like you're starving and dying of thirst if you don't have it— then you'll get it. Paul said, in effect, "I crucify myself so that the Christ essence can live through me. My dreams are no longer mine, they are God's dreams. My desires are no longer mine, they are God's desires, which makes them more rewarding and fulfilling to me than anything I could have come up with. "I have given up everything to know Jesus and the power flowing from his resurrection."

That means doing more than just reading Scripture for ten minutes a day or praying or meditating for an hour once a week. It means getting to the point where the Divine is your food. When the disciples asked Jesus if he was hungry, he said, "I have food that you aren't even aware of." Mystics of many traditions have often gone without food for weeks at a time for the same reason—they get their sustenance on a psychospiritual level that we can barely even conceive of.

Follow the ascent of your spirit up the ladder of the beatitudes. First you're humble; then you mourn over your past faults and failings; then you decide that you want to learn more. Once you learn, you discover how much more there is to know, and you hunger and thirst for still more. When your hunger and thirst reach the breaking point, it's time to go out and act. And what is the first thing that Jesus says you will act on? Be merciful, for you will be shown mercy. Give and you shall receive. Modern authorities on the spiritual life such as Ram Dass and Ken Wilber have observed that genuine enlightenment always manifests as *compassion*—perhaps a better word for mercy—and a desire to be of service to others. Enlightenment is unlikely ever to manifest as the desire to create a huge building fund or to use your followers for your own gain.

The sixth beatitude says, "Blessed are the pure in heart for they will see God." What that really means is that your motives need to be untainted by ego to line up with the Divine will. You may consider yourself to be a terrible sinner, but if you have pure motives, that purity will eventually lead you down the right path, and your inappropriate activities will decrease little by little. Compassion and service are the logical conclusion of spiritual awakening, but you have to be certain that your motivation is on target. Plenty of people meditate and do all kinds of spiritual practices, but because they haven't shed their ego preoccupation first, their practice is all about themselves. That misconception results in deluded teachers who abuse their students, demanding sex and money in exchange for "enlightenment." Their teachings may even be valid in some abstract sense, but if their motives are still egocentric, they will not "see God." They will fail to connect with the Divine, and probably won't enable their students to make that connection either.

In the words of the American Buddhist scholar Robert Thurman, "If you don't dislodge the self-preoccupation core before heavy meditation and retreat, then what you will discover after many years of retreat is how great you are and how you should be preoccupied with yourself! And then you've become a monster. You might be a religious monster, but you'll be a monster."

"Blessed are the peace makers," goes beatitude seven, "for

they shall be called children of God." With purity of motive guiding your acts of compassionate service, you will have no choice but to spread peace in the world. Your very presence will radiate peace to all around you. Here we must understand peace as more than just the cessation of violent, armed conflict, although that is certainly a desirable goal. World peace ultimately derives from inner peace, and so being a peace maker means that every act and every word and even every thought you have comes from a place of inner peace and connectedness with all sentient beings. Negative, unkind, or violent thoughts will destroy the "peace" by creating disruptive spiritual vibrations that, as they accumulate, may eventually manifest as disharmony, a fight, even acts of murder and mayhem. Just listening to negative thoughts or any type of gossip from others destroys the peace. The moment we listen, we're giving our approval, although we express shock or tell ourselves that we don't believe what is being said. If you don't believe what someone is saying, then get up and walk away. Peace, like spiritual practice, requires constant attention.

Finally, "Blessed are those who are persecuted because of righteousness, for theirs is the kingdom of heaven." By the time you arrive at the eighth beatitude, you've climbed the ladder to the top and you will have an attitude that is positive, loving, and filled with peace. It will no longer matter what anyone says or does to you, because you now believe that all things work together for good, and you will not be thrown off center.

I hope this step-by-step exploration has shown you that the beatitudes aren't just eight principles of living, but a whole, organically connected way of life, a Jacob's ladder linking the earthly with the Divine. As with the greatest commandment Jesus named—to love God and love your neighbor as yourself—you can't pick and choose which part of it to obey. You start with humility and sorrow for the mistakes you've made—not self-loathing or self-condemnation—and work your way up the ladder in the power of the Holy Spirit. What if you get to the fourth beatitude and the step breaks and you go tumbling backwards? You start all over again, literally. You become humble and acknowledge that you're not perfect and that you slipped. It takes humility to admit that you made a mistake and you want to get up and start over. Then you express sorrow for the slip and get on with things. It's a little like the thinking behind the 12-Step programs, but instead of taking things one day at a time, you take the ladder of the beatitudes one rung at a time.

About now, you may be wondering what this discourse on the beatitudes is doing in a book about healing. Of course, we shouldn't be surprised to find that everything is interconnected on some level. Yet the Gospel makes it clear just how intimately linked the beatitudes are with healing. As soon as Jesus finished teaching the Sermon on the Mount—which included not only the beatitudes but also his teachings on the primacy of love, the Lord's Prayer, and much more—he came down the mountain and was greeted by a leper. This was a loaded situation to begin with, because scholars tell us that, depending on the nature and severity of their affliction, lepers were forbidden from coming within a certain distance of the general public.

The Gospel account raises the question of why this man was allowed to get so close to the crowd listening to Jesus preach. But if we read Scripture to be transformed, we have to look beneath the literal story to the basic truth it is meant to convey. I believe that whoever wrote this story wanted to get across what the will of God was, and the way he chose was to take one of the most feared diseases of the day and present it in the context of the Sermon on the Mount. The leper was standing close enough to Jesus to hear the words of wisdom in the beatitudes being uttered from the mind and heart of this sacred being. As we have seen, sacred words carry sacred vibrations, especially when they emanate from the heart of love, and those words caused to arise in this poor outcast's heart the belief that all things are possible. So he approached Jesus and said, "Lord, if you want to, you can heal me."

Jesus, of course, replied, "I want to. Be healed."

# Chapter 10

❧ ❧

# *Love Without Judgment: The Ultimate Healer*

he key to the healing of the leper, if not to all of the healing work of Jesus, is the nonjudgmental attitude Jesus brought to it. You could argue that his teachings make all kinds of implicit and sometimes explicit value judgments (although the harshest statements attributed to him are probably later additions). Jesus judges liars and hypocrites along with those who parade their holiness in public or who cling to the letter of the law while denying the spirit. But in his healing words and attitudes, we see nothing the least bit condemnatory. Even his advice to "go thy way and sin no more" can be seen as a spiritual pep talk once we understand the proper translation of *sin* as "missing the mark." When it comes to healing, Jesus may be the least judgmental being ever to have lived. Since this quality of unconditional love is the most important attribute we can bring with us to our healing work—whether for ourselves or for others—we need to understand it as fully as possible.

"Lord," the apostle John said to Jesus one day, "We saw a man casting out demons in your name, and we told him to stop because he was not one of us."

A lot of other religions and healers may help people, the disciples were saying, but they are not doing it with our theology—as if "our" theology has to be correct before God can heal. As Kathryn Kuhlman said so memorably, "There was a time in which my theology was so correct, and there also was a time when there were no miracles." In effect, she decided to leave theology to the theologians. "They are in the business of not having miracles come to pass. I am not, and so I will concentrate on the Holy Spirit and the miracles of God."

Kuhlman's words are similar to what Jesus was teaching. When the disciples complained about those "nondisciples" using Jesus' name to cast out demons, he replied, "Let them go, because if they are not against us, they are with us." He meant that they may approach healing a little differently than you do, or do it with a little different terminology, but their motivation is still love in the Spirit of God. Although Jesus was a devout Jew who followed the Torah and the Jewish traditions of his day, I get the sense that he would have embraced or accepted the wisdom teachings of other religions as well. He lacked the narrowness of mind and heart that characterized even his most loyal disciples. Among the last words of Jesus were, "Father, forgive them, for they know not what they do." Yet the first sermon of Peter after Christ's death places guilt and sin squarely on the Jews who now opposed the nascent Jesus Movement. In almost no time, Peter had already forgotten the Master's last and perhaps greatest teaching.

Nonjudgmental love sounds so simple, but it's so difficult to realize, and without it you will never truly heal anything. The story of the woman at the well in the fourth chapter of the Gospel of John displays a stunning exercise of this kind of love. Jesus stops at a well alone, and when a Samaritan woman comes upon him, he asks her for a drink of water. The woman is shocked, because, as the result of a notorious historic conflict, the Jews would have nothing to do with the Samaritans. But Jesus, knowing how this woman is challenged, shows compassion. He can always put himself in another person's shoes and see how they feel. He tells the Samaritan woman to bring her husband, and she reveals that she is not married. Jesus notes that she speaks truly, because she has had five husbands, nor is she actually married to the man with whom she is now living. But he also knows that if this woman has been married five times and is now living with someone she is not married to, she has undoubtedly been hurt along the way. She is feeling empty, perhaps scorned by her neighbors, and she needs love. So Jesus gives her love without condemning her. He mirrors back to her with no judgment the kind of life she has been leading, so she can see it plainly.

No physical healing takes place in this story, yet when the woman goes back and tells the townfolk what happened, the whole village turns out to hear the teacher. I can easily imagine the rest of the village, prior to this event, saying things that in modern language might go like this: "Did you hear about Sally? You know, she's been married five times. When is this gal going to get her act together? Did you know that Sally is living with a guy she's not even married to? Oh! She ought to be in hell, that rotten woman. I may drink to excess and commit adultery on occasion, but I certainly wouldn't be married five times!"

Jesus never missed an opportunity to practice unconditional love when it was least expected. In a memorable story in the Gospel of Luke (19:1-10), he has entered Jericho and is passing through. A wealthy chief tax collector named Zacchaeus wants to get a look at Jesus, but being short of stature, he can't see over the crowd. So Zacchaeus climbs a sycamore tree and Jesus spots him, looks up and says, "Zacchaeus, come down immediately. I must stay at your house today."

Men like Zacchaeus in those days in Judea were local Jews who collected taxes for the Roman colonial government, taking a cut of the proceeds for themselves. Considered collaborators with the occupying forces, they were among the most despised people in the community. So when the crowd hears what Jesus says, they begin to mutter, "He has gone to be the guest of a sinner." Healing lepers is one thing; having dinner with the enemy is something else again. Zacchaeus is so over-whelmed by the magnitude of Jesus' gesture that he makes an extraordinary gesture of his own. "Look, Lord," he says, "here and now I give half of my possessions to the poor, and if I have cheated anybody out of anything, I will pay back four times the amount." According to Biblical scholars, his offer actually exceeds the requirements of either Jewish or Roman law of that time in cases of fraud. Love begets generosity. "Today salvation has come to this house," Jesus concludes. "For the Son of Man came to seek and to save what was lost."

Today we might say that Jesus "validated" this man who was almost universally loathed by his countrymen. His act of unconditional love healed Zacchaeus of greed and emo-tional constriction, enabling him to open his heart—and his wallet—as never before.

We can learn a great deal just by looking at the three heal-ings I've described: the leper who approached Jesus after the Sermon on the Mount; the Samaritan woman at the well; and Zacchaeus the tax collector. To begin with, all three of them are outcasts, social rejects considered undesirable by their own people for different principles. The leper is a pariah for physical reasons; nobody even wants to come close to him for fear of contracting his disease. He is forced, for the most part, to live in a separate society, apart from the general population, like a prisoner with a life sentence. As a Samaritan, the woman at the well would be considered an outcast by the very people who made up most of Jesus' audi-ence. And although the gospel doesn't specifically say so, her own people must have looked down on her for having had so many husbands and currently living with a man out-side of marriage.

Zacchaeus resides at the other end of the socioeconomic spectrum, but may have suffered more than the first two. Much as we may resist the idea, there is such a thing as rich people's suffering. You have only to glance at the supermarket tabloids (something I'm sure none of us would ever do!) to see how gleefully we tear apart the rich and famous for exhibiting essentially the same foibles many of us have—failing to care adequately for parents or children, adultery, substance abuse, even dressing badly. For all her money, fame, and success, Liz Taylor can't start a new relationship, go on a diet, or make a trip to the hospital without being subjected to the snide laughter and judgment of millions. If you think the rich and famous are so happy, ask yourself why they're such regular visitors to the Betty Ford Clinic.

Although Zacchaeus is at once among the richest and most despised of his people, after one encounter with the unconditional love of Jesus, he exhibits undreamed-of reserves of generosity and humility. That story is particularly affecting because it shows Jesus challenging Zacchaeus in a very direct fashion. "Get down off your high horse," he says in effect, "and serve me."

In two of these three stories, there is no physical healing at all. But the psychological and spiritual healing of all three is momentous. How transformed that Samaritan woman must have been, that she could run back to town and bring the whole village out with her to meet this remarkably nonjudgmental man! There was no "miracle" involved of the kind that might make them say, "Hey, this teacher just made a blind man see. Let's go check it out." The only miracle Jesus performed was to make a woman suffering from severely low self-esteem suddenly feel good about herself. What makes the loving response of Jesus so apt is that this is clearly a woman who has been looking for love all her life, without much success—until now.

The challenge for Zacchaeus, for different reasons, is to acknowledge his own potential for goodness, to which he responds with zest. Imagine yourself today as a Roman Catholic living in Belfast but siding with the Protestants and somehow growing rich from your association. How much stress and anxiety would you be carrying, and how would you bear up under the sheer weight of your neighbors' contempt and implied threats to your safety? Then imagine that the head of the IRA invites himself to dinner at your house, and in front of everyone tells you what a good and noble person you are—and means it. With his Divinely guided intuition, Jesus knows exactly what Zacchaeus needs to heal his psychological suffering. In symbolic language, as Paul said, the body is the temple of the Holy Spirit. Jesus is telling Zacchaeus to get his house in order to prepare for the healing presence of God to dwell within.

In much the same way, the leper is drawn to healing by listening to Jesus speak on the nature of love and selflessness. Something about the language, tone, and look of Jesus infuses this societal reject with the courage suddenly to approach the Master and to say with such confidence, "If you want to, you can heal me." The very way his request is phrased implies that he knows the answer will be yes. The leper gets his wish, but as I've said, the physical healing is less important than the psychological, emotional, and spiritual healings that accompany it. What good is it to heal your physical body anyway, if your emotional life isn't about celebration and joy? Most of us can accept that fame and wealth are no guarantors of happiness or peace of mind, because it has become almost a cliche that money can't buy you love. But neither can physical health bring you love and happiness if you're not also whole mentally, emotionally, and spiritually.

Because unconditional love is so crucial to healing both body and spirit, we need a way to generate this valuable attribute in ourselves that is reasonably practical. If we think in some abstract way that we must love unconditionally, we are likely to abandon the whole enterprise as impossible, because only God and mothers love unconditionally. In my own experience, two approaches have helped more than anything else I know to elicit the capacity for unconditional love that dwells deep inside our spirit, and both are easily within the grasp of anyone reading this book. For many years, I have pondered and meditated on passages of Scripture until an energy was released that motivated me to act in the same way described in those passages. If you read the lives of great saints and mystics such as Hildegard of Bingen, John of the Cross, or Mother Teresa, you'll find that they too used Scripture as their great motivating principle to help them act more like the Christ. (Needless to say, the Scriptures you choose need not be confined to the Hebrew or Christian Bible, but can include the many writings of Buddhist, Hindu, Taoist, Muslim, and other traditions.)

If Jesus were alive, perhaps you could place yourself in his presence and receive the benefit of his unconditional love. Lacking that, reading and repeating his words is the next best thing. In her book *The Dynamic Laws of Prayer* (DeVorss, 1987), Catherine Ponder tells of a school of Christ's followers that was formed in Jerusalem within a decade of his death . . .

". . . whose whole purpose was to understand the sayings of Jesus. The early Christians who studied in that school and who invoked the Christ consciousness by studying the sayings of Jesus went forth repeating his words and parables with such power that they were transformed. And they also transformed the lives of those to whom they ministered. One had only to touch them to be healed. Why did they have such power? Because in addition to other spiritual techniques which they used, they prayed the Lord's Prayer over again and again."

Ponder's explanation for this phenomenon is simple: "Words of truth have life in them."

The second approach I recommend is to make the decision that you will do something good for someone within a prescribed period of time, even if you begin doing so just once a week. It could be as simple as agreeing to do something with a family member or friend that you wouldn't normally do—cooking the kind of meal or going to the kind of movie someone else prefers. It could also mean taking the time to listen to someone—friend, acquaintance, or stranger—who just needs to be listened to. Earlier I spoke about reprogramming through the use of audio- and videotapes, affirmations, and decree. The decision to take action is a form of reprogramming that is both simpler and more difficult to see through, because it requires the will to change.

Fortunately, as I discovered in my own practice over many years, these two approaches feed off each other in a synergistic way that may be the greatest secret pathway to genuine healing. The more you read and repeat the words of Jesus (or any great spiritual master or healer), the more your own consciousness becomes imbued with the spirit of unconditional love. The more that happens, the easier it becomes to do things for other people that you might not ordinarily choose to do, were your concerns about your own comfort to remain uppermost in your consciousness. And the more you do for others, the deeper the spirit of unconditional love will grow within you. This is the most effective way to reprogram yourself from ego-centered consciousness to the Christ consciousness that heals all around it. Just as the leper, the Samaritan woman, and Zacchaeus the tax collector were instantly reprogrammed because of exposure to the unconditional love of Jesus, so it can happen for you if you follow this simple prescription.

# Epilogue

*⌒⌒⌒*

*I* find it fitting to end on a note of prescription, because this book is not intended to be a scholarly or theoretical work about medicine or religion. Rather, it is a guide to help you take the simple healing principles that I have presented here into your life and apply them on a daily basis. My goal is to lead you to experience life and healing instead of just studying about it. To that end, I recommend supplementing the exercises I've incorporated into the text with the many audiotapes I've created over the past few years. You may also draw on all of the exercises related to prayer and healing that appear in the series of books I've written with Peter Occhiogrosso.

But whether you use this book alone or in concert with my other books and tapes, I hope that it will have a practical effect on your physical, emotional, and spiritual health. If you feel you have received help from it in any way, please e-mail me and tell me your story, as your experience may serve to inspire others who face similar circumstances. For that same reason, I would like to share the testimonies of a few of the people who have received Divine healing through the vehicle of my services. Because they've expressed a wish to preserve their privacy, I have identified them only by their initials, but rest assured that theirs are sincere accounts of healing. Some of the statements below were extracted from interviews conducted by my medical team following one of my healing services. Others are taken from letters written or e-mailed to me by people who attended one of my healing workshops or services. I hope they may inspire you to believe that healing of all sorts is not only possible but probable, as long as you remain open to it.

### J. A. C., Australia (excerpted from interview):

*I was somewhat hesitant to stand up at first, because I was feeling that others should go before me. At the time I was suffering from scoliosis, lordosis, and various misalignments of the spine. The medical people attending the Intensive confirmed this diagnosis from my doctor before Ron began to work with me.*

*Ron asked me to sit in a chair and stood behind me, saying that he would say a few calming words. Then he commanded the situation to fix itself! He just said, "Align and fix." For the first few minutes, I didn't experience any sensations, but after a few more minutes, I started to feel some movement in my right hip. I felt tingling and motion in that area as if things were cracking— almost like having a body manipulation by a chiropractor or something. I heard a crack in my lumbar area, following which my neck started to tingle and move where I had always had problems with the fifth and sixth cervical vertebrae. I began to cough up phlegm as if I were having a bronchial attack.*

*After a few minutes, I was feeling better and the tingling stopped. Ron asked the medical people to examine me again. They reported that the vertebrae had realigned, and the lordosis had virtually disappeared. This was consistent with my own sensation of where the actual position for my hips and pelvis were in relation to the rest of my body. I was standing in a different position from the*

*way I had done for the past 42 years. I now have a full
range of motion with no impediments, and the intermit-
tent pain is gone. I am experiencing absolutely no medical
symptoms whatever.*

*My understanding of what happened is clear. I have
definitely experienced a spiritual healing from the Divine.
It doesn't surprise me; in fact, it pleases me enormously!
I felt very strongly that I was drawn to Ron's conference
for a reason.*

**J.B., California** (excerpted from interview):

*I was in a car accident over 13 years ago, and have
since experienced constant pain, primarily on the left side
of my body, where I am also stiff. Right after the accident,
I was having up to 25 seizures a day, but that number
decreased over time. In 1992, I was diagnosed with multi-
ple sclerosis. My inability to walk distances has required
the use of a cane. Recently, my vision decreased tremendously again. All of this is documented by my many
physicians, and I had just about given up on the traditional route for healing.*

*I do believe in the power of prayer, and there have
been many prayers through the years culminating, I
know, in this week. The week before I came here, however,
I thought I might have to cancel, because I dislocated my
hip. I didn't think that I could endure the pain riding the
train here. I prayed that somehow I would manage. I
arrived here in tremendous pain, but I knew I was in the
right place.*

*I experienced my healing with Ron during the
evening Forgiveness Ceremony. I could really feel my
heart beating. I could feel the whole organ, the shape, the
big volume of my heart, as though that was the only part
of my body. Then there was no pain, and my back became
straight and my hips perfect. I no longer have pain on my*

*left side or anywhere. I can also sleep now. I used to miss three to four days of sleep because of my fibromyalgia, but now I sleep all night through. This, in itself, is a miracle to me.*

*I have so much to be thankful for. Ron has touched my soul. I've been in church my whole life, but he has taught me things I've never heard coming from such a level of love—love and joy without exclusion. I am pleased.*

### B.B., California (e-mail):

*I had a healing experience at this current workshop, but the one I want to share is from a workshop with Ron that I attended several months ago. A friend of mine who wasn't at Ron's conference has been suffering from various kinds of cancer for the last five or six years. She recovered from esophageal cancer and then came down with a cancer of the throat that was unrelated. While she was in the middle of her treatment for that cancer, she started to become more physically ill, weak, and unable to eat. She was more or less giving up hope and checking out. Her husband called me a few days after I got back from the previous workshop and said that his wife really needed to see me. I went right over and took with me Ron's* Healing Prayers *tape. When I was working with her, I had a feeling that I needed to command something, and then some kind of energy would bring her back [from the brink of death].*

*I have a private practice in the health-care field and am experienced in the healing arts. This time, however, something came over me that was different from what I normally experience. I'm not sure what it was, but I believe it was the Holy Spirit. When I saw this woman lying there, I felt a combination of panic and compassion. I knew something big had to happen to pull her back. I put my hand on her head and I just made the invocation,*

*"Come, Holy Spirit," and prayed that whatever she needed would come through. Her husband was there, and he was also feeling very afraid, overwhelmed, and exhausted. I had him sit with his wife and hold her hand so that I could work on them simultaneously. When I finished, I gave them a homework assignment of listening to Ron's healing prayers every day while holding hands. She completely recovered within a day of that experience. She went from being ready to leave her body to actually feeling renewed, refreshed, and wanting to live. She is back at work now and continues to recover.*

*The critical thing I learned from Ron was that I was able to have energy work through me that was bigger than myself. I also feel that the woman was able to make the choice to come back to her body because of Ron's prayers and my being there. And I saw how the commanding invocation of the Holy Spirit can change anything.*

*As for my healing at this workshop, Ron worked on my shoulder joint that has been torn for about four years. I've had pain from it for all these years, but it had been getting worse over the last two days. The pain has been very discouraging. I believe that the first thing he did was to pull out the fear I've had over this. When he touched me, I felt a vibration, then he gave me a homework assignment to work on moving my shoulder. I'm in the middle of it, and it is actually hurting a lot, so I'm sure it's working itself through. From my experience, I can tell that I'm having a healing crisis, because it's hurting more than when he first started. It's a good thing because everything locked in there is moving out. My arm, right now, has an increase in its range of motion. This is just remarkable.*

**M.M., California** (letter):

*Dear Ron,*

*My husband and I and our parents want to thank you so much for the healing you did on the 22nd of May for our parents, who were visiting from Japan, especially for my husband's mother and my father. My mother-in-law had been suffering from osteoarthritic pain in her knees and lower back for 20 years. Conventional medical doctors gave her medications that didn't help much. Acupuncture and moxibustion [herbal heat treatment] helped reduce her pain by 30 to 40 percent, which lasted about a week after each treatment. But she could not receive it often enough because of the distance she had to travel to the treatment center. Before she saw you, she used to use a cane even inside the house, and keep her body bent at a right angle to minimize pain.*

*During the healing, she felt an electric shock-like sensation rush through her fingers. Immediately after your healing was done, her pain was gone and she could stand straight and started to walk without a cane. After she realized that the pain had disappeared, she could not help crying because she felt so grateful. Even though she experienced a slight setback after she went back to Japan, she says that she feels 80 percent better than before she saw you. She is very happy that she does not have to use the cane inside the house anymore. She can also do more things with much less discomfort because of the reduced pain and better posture. She is a Buddhist/Shintoist and has a strong faith in God, which we think maximized the healing power.*

*My father, who had prostate cancer for five years, said that after the healing service, he felt something change in his body. At last month's checkup, his PSA [prostate specific antigen] number had increased, but he's feeling good physically, and his urination is becoming less frequent during the night. For five months now, he hasn't had leg pain due to the metastasis of prostate cancer, something he used to experience before the healing.*

*The whole family went through spiritual transformations from the healing. My in-laws started to meditate every morning with your healing tape. My parents got interested in reading books on spirituality and are planning to start meditation. My husband and I were inspired and uplifted by seeing God's power flowing through you in front of our eyes. Even my husband's brother in Japan, who never saw your healing, felt inspired, and his faith in God enhanced after hearing our stories. We feel so grateful to the Divine Mother for her grace and love. We heard that you are a disciple of Paramahansa Yogananda; so are my husband and I. Now we understand why we were attracted to you and why this wonderful opportunity was given to us. Master guided us to you! I thank you greatly for the healing of all of us.*

### B. M., California (letter):

*Dear Ron,*

*When you visited Unity of Tustin, in California, I was overwhelmed with a horrendous skin disease called pityriasis rubra pilaris (PRP) [a skin disorder causing persistent inflammation and scaling of the skin, with no known cause], which completely covered all of my skin from head to toe. Thanks to your visit, I enjoyed a miraculous healing. PRP is a rare chronic disease that lasts up to three years and for which there is no known cure. My skin shed daily, somewhat like a snake molting. Because my skin would not hold my body heat, I was wearing winter clothes and an overcoat inside my office just to stay warm. The palms of my hands were thick like leather, and the soles of my feet were cracking, which made walking a challenge. I was living life asking myself, "Can I get through today?"*

*Eight months into the disease, I was doing everything medically possible and recovering ever so slowly. I was seeing a noted specialist at the University of California at Irvine who treats PRP. I was also seeing vibrational healers and an accomplished herbalist/acupuncturist.*

*Within 12 hours of attending your healing church service and laying-on-of-hands workshop, my recovery was in high gear. I attended with an open mind but with no expectations. Within four months, I was completely healed from PRP. The specialist I was seeing could not believe the incredible healing I was experiencing and called it "miraculous."*

*Your healing service, in which you called on the healing power of God, saved me from perhaps another two years of absolute misery. I thank you for bringing the healing power of God into my life.*

**S.G., California** (letter):

*It has been almost a year since I first heard about Ron Roth, and I now have difficulty remembering who I was before then. Just thinking about all the remarkable changes and experiences I've had leaves me speechless, in awe, and almost in tears.*

*It all started one day when I happened to be thumbing through a magazine, and there in front of me was a picture of Ron Roth. There was information with the picture about where he would be appearing next, which, to my delight, was the very next weekend here in Southern California. I had no idea what to expect, but I do remember looking forward to whatever this seminar had in store for me. First of all, I never expected to have so much fun. Ron was so funny that he made it easy for me not only to understand what he was teaching, but also to absorb* everything. Everything that was happening in that room felt so natural to me, especially the wonderful prayers he said with and for us.

Toward the end, I felt disappointed that it was almost over. Little did I know that it wasn't over for me. During the last prayer, I began to feel a rotating, warm, and loving sensation in my heart. Eventually we were invited up to have Ron touch everyone's temples. When it was my turn, he whispered something to do with ten years ago. As he touched my temples, I instantly saw (not with my eyes) a beautiful bright white light swoop into my body and out through the top of my head. Right after that, I remember falling back as if there were clouds behind me ready to catch my fall.

That evening, I felt so light and focused that it took time to realize that a neck injury I had received months ago had disappeared completely. It had been so bad that I was unable to raise my head above nose level. It was hard to believe it was really gone. I didn't even have to concentrate on it—it just happened!

A few days later, still feeling as if I were walking on clouds, I was parked in my car when all of a sudden I began to feel a powerful love sensation taking over my entire being. It was so powerful that I literally could not see or hear anything around me. There are no words in our vocabulary to describe this feeling. Needless to say, I do know without a doubt that there is a wonderful God with us, loving us and guiding us every minute of every day.

My journey continues. I have managed to collect just about every audiotape of Ron's to help me keep on track, and I have attended almost all of his seminars in Northern and Southern California, which have brought about some life-changing experiences in me. After his San Francisco seminar in May, for example, I had just returned home when I began to massage my daughter's semi-

*deformed feet as I was putting her to bed. Her feet slant inward with a protruding bone jutting out. Normally, every time I rubbed her feet, my heart would break. Except this one night, when I remembered Ron's healing words of prayer, which were simply, "Come, Holy Spirit." I said these words with all my heart and trusted in God.*

*The next day, I did not think about the previous night until evening, when my family and I returned from walking our dogs. My daughter walked in the door, kicked off her shoes as usual, and stopped in her tracks! She looked down at her feet and yelled, "Mommy, look, my feet are straight!" That instant, I ran with tears to another room and thanked God from the bottom of my heart. Later that evening, I explained to my daughter as best I could that God's love for her had healed her feet. She was very surprised and cried tears of joy.*

### C.M., Illinois (letter):

*Dear Ron,*

*For 16 years I suffered from endometriosis [an infection of the uterine lining]. My symptoms included pelvic pain, heavy bleeding, sometimes fatigue and painful intercourse all month long. I had a laparatomy to remove cysts that were inside both ovaries and was told that my uterus looked as if someone had taken a shotgun to it. To help shrink the endometriosis, I was placed on two hormonal treatments and was informed that it was very unlikely that I could ever become pregnant. Prior to the Spring Intensive, I was preparing to have further surgery to control the worsening symptoms. My doctor said that I would most likely need to have a hysterectomy.*

*At the Spring Intensive, I was completely healed of endometriosis! During the empowerment service, I went up to you, and you placed your hand on my forehead and said, "Heal, restore, empower." A recent examination by*

my doctor showed no trace of endometriosis, and I will
not have to have any surgery! It literally feels as if my old
reproductive system was thrown away and I was given a
new one. In my heart, I know I now have the ability to
have children and to create life anew on all levels of my
being and in all areas of my life.

Thank you, thank you, God; and thank you, Ron.
Namaste.

### R. H., Maryland (e-mail):

Dear Ron,

I wanted to write you and thank you for the commitment you have made to work with folks like me, who have
committed to follow a spiritual path. I realized this week
what a profound sense of gratitude I have for you because
of the opportunity to study and learn from you. I feel
truly blessed in having had these experiences with you
both this year and last, plus all of the other hours of learning that I have received through your tapes and books. I
want you to know that I feel a very special heart connection with you for all you have given me. I have shared in
the essence of who you are, and I am indeed richer for it.

I wanted to share some of what happened to me during the last Intensive. My experience during the healing
of my back was quite profound. I was not able to fully
comprehend what had happened at the time of the healing
itself and, frankly, I think that I did not believe anything
had really happened until later in the day. I had been told
by two doctors, based on x-rays, that I had a 15 percent
curvature of the spine and that I would have to wear a
three-quarter-inch lift for my left leg for the rest of my
life. For over 17 years since a bad car accident in 1982,
I've tried to make the best of this, but have always had
some level of pain and discomfort. I've been to see over
25 doctors through the years and have tried every known

type of therapy, including more than 100 shots in my back over a four-year period. I have been in traction, had acupuncture, physical manipulation, psychological evaluations, body wraps, massage, and have hung by my ankles, to name just a few treatments. In the last three years, because of exercising, I experienced pain only two or three days a week instead of every day. What I have learned most profoundly from this experience is that I had to ask for healing even though my condition was not life-threatening and even though there were dozens of others present who might be more in need of healing than I. The process of asking for healing and then receiving it was life-changing.

During the healing, there was an immediate release on the left side of my body, and my husband, Bruce, who was holding my legs, did notice the left leg "let go." Several people in the audience said they saw the leg release. I had trouble fully accepting the healing. "What is this?" my intellect shouted. Had I wished for the healing so hard that I made the release happen, and would it last? When I left the room at break, I went out by myself to the woods. I tried to balance on both legs and could do so perfectly, something which I had not been able to do since the accident. The absolute indication of healing came when I realized that my habit of "holding my body," which I have done for more than 17 years, was gone. I felt empty, void, and vulnerable. What would I replace the pain with? The loss of the need to hold myself together and in balance felt strange. While by myself, I asked God to replace that large, empty space with compassion for others. This process more than anything else signified to me that I had been healed.

I didn't wear the lift in my shoe the day of the healing and felt the keen sensation of being fully in balance. I laughed and was deeply grateful. The next day, just as a silly test, I tried my lift on in the morning and instanta-

*neously, the old familiar pain returned. I heard quite clearly, as if another were speaking to me, "Okay, if you want to pretend you have not been healed, go right ahead." I even asked my husband if he had said something to me, but he had not. I took the lift out of my shoe and have not worn it since. I have had no pain, no sense of imbalance, and I am still adjusting to the freedom of being in balance and the feeling of having been healed. I can't speak about this to others very effectively, because it seems unspeakably miraculous. It takes my breath away to think of this blessing I have received.*

*One other experience, which surpassed this healing and anything else I have ever experienced, occurred during the darshan ceremony at this same Intensive. From the moment you entered the room for that service, I felt a rush of energy throughout my body. I could hardly walk up to greet you and was grateful to return to my seat. I spent the next two hours alternately on the floor and in my seat, unable to come out of a deep communion with the Holy Spirit. I felt that someone had plugged me into a high-voltage current. As this experience continued of its own accord, I recognized female energy. In my own private meditation, energy vibrations had been present, but these were qualitatively different. This was a new presence, and all I can say is that it was female. During mediation the day before, I had experienced Mother Mary and Jesus anointing me as a healer, the day of my ordination, and it felt like this presence was coming back to be with me, although I didn't know whether it was Mother Mary or the Holy Spirit.*

*Thirty minutes after the darshan service ended, I still could not move. I asked this presence if we might meet again and She said, "Yes." Then I smelled the powerful scent of roses permeating the room. When I finally arose to approach the altar for prayer, I realized that all the rose petals from the ceremony were gone. Not one petal was left in the room, but the powerful smell of roses was intoxicating. I have never in all my life had such an experience, and may never again. It was uniquely designed for me, because if I had been my normal rational self, I would not have gotten the message. I think this experience was designed for me to learn that the Holy Spirit is present in our lives, that healing happens in the Holy Spirit's time frame alone, that healing is completely in the Holy Spirit's hands, that I am merely a facilitator when I help others, and that this powerful connection will always be there for me. You are among the very few with whom I can share this. I realized that I was a doubting Thomas in a female body asking for irrefutable evidence, even though I deeply wished that I was somewhere else spiritually.*

*Later in the day when I was wondering aloud about why this powerful experience had happened at this particular time in my life, a clairvoyant spoke to me and said that she had a message for me. She said that this Spiritual Being had not been able to come any sooner because I had been too out of balance. I laughed out loud, given what had happened at the physical healing. (The clairvoyant knew almost nothing about the specifics of my physical healing from the day before.) Mother Mary, or the feminine part of the Holy Spirit, connected with me again the very next day, as I had asked. I remain humbled beyond words. Thinking about this now as time has passed, I realize that the side of my body that has always hurt and was shorter overall was the left side. In energy medicine, this is regarded as the feminine side of the body. I felt as though She was restoring my feminine energy to wholeness so that I could go forward in balance physically, emotionally, and spiritually.*

*Since these experiences and my ordination, people are increasingly calling to come see me about spiritual heal-*

*ing. I feel I have finally "come home." I have the rest of my lifetime to learn more about these things. I am deeply grateful for the love and learning you have shared with me, enabling me to receive three such precious gifts: the physical healing, the communion with the Holy Spirit, and my ordination as a spiritual healer.*

*God's continued blessing on your work.*

# About Ron Roth, Ph.D.

**Ron Roth, Ph.D.**, is an internationally known teacher, spiritual healer, and modern-day mystic. He has appeared on many television and radio programs, including *The Oprah Winfrey Show*. Ron is the author of several books, including the bestseller *The Healing Path of Prayer* and the audiocassette *Healing Prayers*. He served in the Roman Catholic priesthood for more than 25 years and is the founder of Celebrating Life Institute in Peru, Illinois, where he lives.

ოია

# About Peter Occhiogrosso

**Peter Occhiogrosso** has been a journalist for over 30 years and has written or co-written many books about world religion and spirituality, including his popular guide to the world's great religious traditions, *The Joy of Sects*. He also co-authored *The Healing Path of Prayer, Prayer and the Five Stages of Healing,* and *Holy Spirit: The Boundless Energy of God* with Ron Roth. You can learn more about Peter at his Website: **joyofsects.com**. His e-mail address is: **peteroc@prodigy.net**.

ოია

For more information on Ron Roth's Spiritual Healing Retreats, Holistic Spirituality Five-Day Intensives, Workshops, and Seminars, or to send in your Prayer Request and be placed on his mailing list, please use the address below:

Celebrating Life!
P.O. Box 428
Peru, IL 61354
e-mail: **ronroth@theramp.net**
Fax: 815-224-3395

Please visit Ron Roth's website at: **ronroth.com**.

# The Following Materials Are Available Through Celebrating Life

## BOOKS

*The Healing Path of Prayer,* with Peter Occhiogrosso

## AUDIOCASSETTES

*Celebrate Life: Choices That Heal,* with Paul Funfsinn
*Divine Dialogue: How to Reclaim Your Spiritual Power*
*Forgiveness Therapy: A Christ-Centered Approach*
*Heal Your Life: Consciousness and Energy Medicine*
*Healing Meditation and Affirmations*
*Invoking the Sacred,* with Caroline Myss, Ph.D.
*Prayer and Spirit As Energy Medicine*
*Reclaiming Your Spiritual Power*
*Spiritual Exploration: Navigating the Dark Night,*
with Caroline Myss, Ph.D.
*Taking Control of Your Life's Direction*
*The Biology of Prayer,* with Caroline Myss, Ph.D.
*The Lord's Prayer: Teachings on the Our Father in Aramaic*
*The Path to Answered Prayer*
*Transformed by Love: The Healing Power of Authentic Self-Love*

## VIDEOCASSETTES

*Praying with Power for Healing Guidance, Abundance and Relationships*
*Spiritual Healing: Merging Mysticism and Meditation with Medicine*

## ADDITIONAL TOOLS FOR HEALING
(designed by Ron Roth)

Essential Oil: "Mystical Rose." Ingredients: Pure Rose, Sandalwood, Amber, and Musk

Mala Prayer Beads Bracelet: Eleven Quality Gemstones with instructions

**Coming Soon:** *Healing Prayer Cards*

# Other Hay House Titles of Related Interest

## BOOKS

*The Experience of God*, edited by Jonathan Robinson

*Experiencing the Soul*, by Eliot Jay Rosen

*God, Creation, and Tools for Life*, by Sylvia Browne

*Handle with Prayer*, by Alan Cohen

*The Jesus Code*, by John Randolph Price

*7 Paths to God*, by Joan Borysenko, Ph.D.

## AUDIOS

*All about God*, a Dialogue Between Neale Donald Walsch and Deepak Chopra, M.D.

*Healing with the Angels*, by Doreen Virtue, Ph.D.

*Pathways to God*, a Dialogue Between Joan Borysenko, Ph.D., and Deepak Chopra, M.D.

(All of the above titles are available at your local bookstore, or may be ordered by calling the numbers on the last page.)

❦ ❧

We hope you enjoyed this Hay House book.
If you would like to receive a free catalog featuring
additional Hay House books and products, or if
you would like information about the
Hay Foundation, please contact:

Hay House, Inc.
P.O. Box 5100
Carlsbad, CA 92018-5100

**(760) 431-7695** or **(800) 654-5126**
**(760) 431-6948 (fax)** or **(800) 650-5115 (fax)**

Please visit the Hay House Website at: **hayhouse.com**

❦ ❧